Sempringham Studies

Italy 1915-1940

Philip Morgan

Sempringham publishing, Bedford

Cover picture: The front cover of a Fascist youth journal (Mary Evans Picture Library, London).

Other illustrations: *Illustrated London News* pp. 16, 22, 29, 68 and 72; Mary Evans Picture Library pp. 17, 34 and 50; *Daily Herald* 12 June 1940 p. 41; *Il Popolo d'Italia* p. 66; *Eeleftheron Vema* 2 November 1940 p. 71.
The publisher will be glad to make suitable arrangements with any copyright holders whom it has not been possible to contact.

Sempringham Books are available (post free) to schools, colleges and individuals direct (10% discount on orders of 10 or more of the same title): Sempringham Books, PO Box 248, Bedford MK40 2SP.

Sempringham Books are distributed to booksellers by
Central Books, 99 Wallis Road, London E9 5LN   Tel. 0181-986 4854.

Contents

To student readers and their tutors

Ways to use this book

This book covers a period of great activity. It spans Italian History from the First World War until Italy's participation in the Second and it traces how Italian society, and one man in particular, Benito Mussolini, sought to deal with the issues created by economic, social and ideological development from the latter part of the nineteenth century within a Western liberal ideology.

The need to effectively and rapidly assimilate a topic studied for the first time or to see a topic, previously studied at a lower level, with fresh eyes when studied at a higher level underlay the arrangement of this volume. The core of the book, Chapters 5 to 9, present the events of these years with a narrative focus. Students and their tutors are aware that narrative is not enough for success with advanced study so that is why the core chapters are buttressed by Chapters 1 and 2 at the beginning and 11 and 12 at the end to provide perspective and to encourage analysis as well as sound student assessment and judgement of the topic. For further guidelines on how to use information to develop analysis and prepare essay answers consult Chapters 4, 6 and 7 of *The Good History Students' Handbook*, Edited by Gilbert Pleuger (Sempringham, 1993) or Chapters 3, 6 and 7 of *Undergraduate History Study - The Guide to Success* (Sempringham, 1997).

How a book is used will be dependent on students' study purpose. It is seldom the best procedure to read a textbook in a uniform way from beginning to end. Students who use this volume as a primary introductory text will absorb, by reading and noting, the relevant parts of the core chapters but in order to benefit most from those chapters the first and last two chapters should be skim read and the key issues noted. An overall survey of events can be gained by a scan of the three-page Chronology, pages 2-4. A quick glance at the Glossary will inform on central terms before the Chapters 5 to 9 are read.

The core chapters challenge greater attention to detail. To identify the main issues, the Questions to Consider at the end of

the chapter should be referred to before the chapter is tackled,
thereby the mind is prepared to notice the main issues.

Chapter subheadings will help with note structure. Not all parts of
a chapter need to be noted in the same depth and detail. With a
chapter completed, the reader will be able to provide responses to
the Questions to Consider. These responses will provide much of
the substance to answers to all but a few course and examination
questions.

Chapter 3 provides brief biographies of five of the men who had
most influence in this period of Italian History and Chapter 11
provides a historiographical survey, especially helpful for
questions which require this dimension.

History study now requires work with documents. In Chapters 4
to 9 there are 21 carefully-selected, concise documents, extracts
placed to be in the appropriate position in the text. This placement
enables readers to contextualise the document, a requirement of
document work. By reference to the text, comprehension of the
document and its tone is furthered as well as encouragement to
appreciate the strengths and weaknesses of the document - all of
which will refine skills with this aspect of advanced History study.

1 Overview and Issues

On his appointment as Prime Minister in October 1922, the leader of the Fascist movement, Benito Mussolini, reportedly said to the King, 'I bring you the Italy of Vittorio Veneto', a reference to the Italian army's final victory over the Austrians in the First World War four years earlier. In June 1940, Mussolini, now *Duce* of the Fascist regime, declared war on France and Britain and invaded France. The enemies of 1915-18 were the allies of 1940 and vice-versa. But the two world wars provide the only suitable framework for understanding the Fascist period of contemporary Italian history.

The Fascist movement drew its ideas, values and methods from Italy's wartime experience, and attempted to recruit its members among the young soldiers returning from the trenches. Fascism's political opportunity came as the result of the country's post-war crisis in 1919-20. This crisis arose out of the divisive impacts of the war on a scarcely united people, many of whom did not feel that their first or ultimate loyalty was to Italy and certainly had little attachment to and belief in the political class and institutions of the national state after its creation in 1871. The Fascist 'totalitarian' regime which developed from the mid-1920s was an attempt to bridge the gap between the State and the people by means of force, organisation and propaganda, to 'nationalise' Italians so that, in Mussolini's words, 'tomorrow Italian and Fascist, rather like Italian and Catholic, mean the same thing'.

In this sense, Fascism was *one* response to *the* issue in Italy after political and territorial unification in 1871: how to forge a feeling of nationhood and national identity and community among people separated from each other throughout their history by class, religion, region and locality, and political ideologies. For Fascism, war was both means and end, the way of achieving its aims and also an aim in itself. War was the only way in which Italy could expand her territory and become a Great Power and the only way the country could finally be made 'Fascist' or 'Fascistised'. A strong and united people was both the essential condition for fighting a successful war and the outcome of such a war. Mussolini described the Fascist 'totalitarian' state as an 'ethical' state, meaning that the State was not 'neutral', simply providing a framework of law and order in which people could go about their lives undisturbed. It had 'values' which it was responsible for impressing on the population at large, and therefore intervened in the way people behaved and ran their lives. The aim of the 'totalitarian' state was, indeed, to take over people's lives and to prepare Italians for war, the great 'educator' and test of the nation and national cohesion.

Chronological Table

1914

Aug   First World War starts; Italy remains neutral.
Nov   Mussolini founds his newspaper, *Il Popolo d'Italia*, and is expelled from the Socialist party.

1915

May   Italy enters the war on the side of Britain and France.

1917

Oct-Nov   Battle of Caporetto.

1918

Oct-Nov   Battle of Vittorio Veneto.
Nov   Armistice is signed.

1919

Jan   The Catholic Italian Popular party is formed.
March   Mussolini forms the first *fascio di combattimento* at Milan.
June   Francesco Nitti becomes Prime Minister.
         Treaty of Versailles is signed.
Sept   Gabriele D'Annunzio occupies Fiume.
Nov   Parliamentary elections.

1920

June   Giolitti becomes Prime Minister.
Aug-Sept   Workers occupy factories in the north.

1921

Jan   Italian Communist party is formed.
May   Parliamentary elections; Mussolini and another 35 Fascists are elected.
Nov   The National Fascist party is created.

1922

Feb   Pius XI becomes Pope.
Oct   The 'March on Rome'; Mussolini becomes Prime Minister.
Nov   Mussolini is given emergency powers by parliament for a year.
Dec   The Fascist Militia is created.

1923

Jan   The Fascist Grand Council is created.
Aug   Mussolini orders the occupation of Corfu.

1924

April   Parliamentary elections take place under the Acerbo Law.
June   The socialist deputy, Giacomo Matteotti, is murdered; opposition parties boycott parliament.

1925

Jan   Mussolini declares the Fascist dictatorship.
Oct   The 'battle for grain' is launched.

1926

April   The Fascist syndical laws are approved.
July   The Ministry of Corporations is created.
Nov   Special dictatorial decrees are issued.

1927

Dec   The revaluation of the *lira* is achieved.

1928

Dec   The Fascist Grand Council is made a constitutional body.

1929

Feb   The Lateran Pacts are signed.

1931

Dec   Achille Starace becomes PNF Secretary.

1932

Oct   The Fascist regime celebrates the 10th anniversary of Fascism's coming to power; the PNF reopens its ranks to new members.

1934

Feb   Corporations are created.
June   Mussolini and Hitler meet for the first time at Venice.
July   Nazis murder the Austrian Chancellor, Engelbert Dollfuss; Mussolini defends Austrian independence.

1935

Oct   Italy invades Ethiopia, and League of Nations sanctions are imposed against Italy.

1936

May   Mussolini declares victory in Ethiopia.
June   Mussolini's son-in-law, Galeazzo Ciano, is appointed Foreign Minister.

Oct   Mussolini declares the formation of the Rome-Berlin Axis; Italy and Germany agree to intervene on Franco's side in the Spanish Civil War.

1938

March   Hitler unites Austria with Germany, with Mussolini's approval.
July   Anti-Jewish laws are adopted.
Sept   The Munich Conference.

1939

April   Italy occupies Albania.
May   Italy and Germany sign the Pact of Steel.
Sept   Germany invades Poland, and Britain and France declare war on Germany; Italy says that it is a 'non-belligerent'.

1940

June   Italy enters the war on Germany's side, and invades France.
Oct   Italy attacks Greece.

1942

Nov   Allies land in North Africa.

1943

March   Workers strike in northern Italy.
July   Allies land in Sicily.
            The Fascist Grand Council meets and decides to end Mussolini's leadership; Mussolini is arrested by the King, and Badoglio becomes Prime Minister.
Sept   Allies land on the Italian mainland; Italy announces an armistice and declares war on Germany; the Germans occupy Italy; the King and Badoglio flee to the south; armed anti-Fascist Resistance begins; Mussolini is rescued by the Germans and put at the head of the Salò Republic.

1945

April   Northern Italy is liberated; Mussolini is captured and executed by partisans.

1946

June   Italy decides to abolish the monarchy in a referendum.

1948

Jan   The Italian Republic is officially in existence.

2 Italy 1871-1915

The question of forming a national community, where the bulk of the population felt some sense of loyalty to and identity with the nation, was one relevant to all European countries in the late nineteenth century, not just to the new national states in central and southern Europe, Germany and Italy. It is noticeable, for instance, that France and Britain, hardly new countries in the way Germany and Italy were, introduced systems of mass compulsory and free primary level education at about the same time as the German and Italian governments did after 1871. The French term for school teacher was *instituteur*, and schools in these countries were seen as one of the most important formative influences on children, the places where teachers, using the standard national language rather than dialect and teaching a curriculum which included 'civics' as well as 'national' subjects like history and geography, would literally 'institute' the nation.

In Italy, the process of forming the nation did not proceed smoothly. For one thing, Italy was politically and territorially unified in 1871 for the first time since the sixth century, when barbarian invasions destroyed the political unity of the country achieved under the Roman Republic and Empire. When nineteenth century nationalist politicians looked to Italy's past to find hope,

The fascio littorio *(literally meaning 'lictor's bundle') was the official symbol of the Fascist movement and the Fascist State, here used on a book cover. In ancient Rome, officials called 'lictors' accompanied the chief magistrates in processions carrying the bundle of rods bound up with an axe, its blade protruding, as a sign of the magistrates' authority. The symbol was one way in which the Fascist regime used the idea of* Romanitá *(Roman-ness') in all its public displays, quite deliberately saying that Fascism was the re-creation of the glorious past of Imperial Rome*

justification and models of a united Italy, they could find nothing in over 1500 years of Italian history except foreign invasion and rule, regional states often at war with each other and using and being used by foreign states in internal and international power struggles. The Fascists claimed that they were completing the *Risorgimento* by binding the masses to the State. But significantly the official myth of the Fascist regime, which inspired the symbols and rituals of its organisations and public ceremonies, was the ancient Roman tradition, marking the power, unity, collective discipline and civilisation of empire. The lack of a recognised central political authority in Italy over centuries was one reason why local civic pride and identity was more developed among most Italians than any sense of national belonging. The governments of the newly-unified single state of Italy faced the problem of getting Italians used to this new state when most of them had lived in separate Italian states often with different systems of rule. Almost inevitably, people identified the new state with the introduction of national policies, like military service and higher taxes, which made them feel that life was better or less bad under previous rulers.

The Political System

The minority coming from the educated and propertied middle class and liberal aristocracy who had wanted unification and became the country's new rulers, were aware of the fact that the bulk of the population had not participated in the process of national unification, largely achieved through the successful local wars and European diplomacy of the north-western Italian kingdom of Piedmont. They put aside any thoughts of giving Italy a federal political system, where power was shared between central and regional governments as in Germany, which some nationalists considered was better suited to the local and regional identities prevalent in the country. Instead, they imposed a very centralised political and administrative system based on the way the dominant Italian state, Piedmont, had been governed, precisely because they thought that only tight control from the centre was capable of holding together a varied and disunited nation. The argument for centralisation was reinforced by the Italian army's effective occupation of much of the south of the country between 1860 and 1865, in order to put down the usual banditry and crime which were inflamed by peasants' resistance to the demands of the new state and encouraged by the rulers who had lost their positions in the new kingdom.

The Catholic Church

The Catholic Church was perceived to be the major obstacle to the national unity and stability of the new Italy. Unification was achieved at the expense of the Pope's own state in Rome and central Italy which he, like his predecessors as head of the Catholic Church saw as a guarantee of the Church's independence from any earthly power and hence essential for him to carry out his

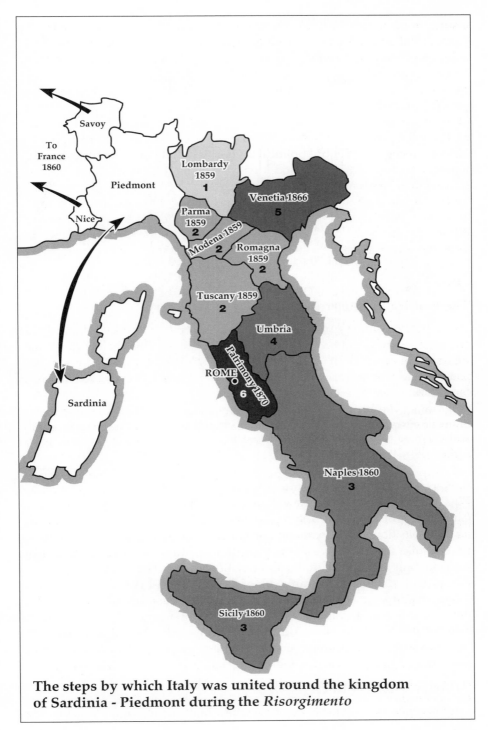

The steps by which Italy was united round the kingdom of Sardinia - Piedmont during the *Risorgimento*

Italian general elections, 1870-1946

	eligible to vote	% of population	actual voters	% of eligible voters
1870	530,000	2.0	241,000	45.5
1874	572,000	2.1	319,000	55.7
1876	605,000	2.2	358,000	59.2
1880	622,000	2.2	370,000	59.4
1882	2,018,000	6.9	1,224,000	60.7
1886	2,420,000	8.1	1,416,000	58.5
1890	2,753,000	9.0	1,477,000	53.7
1892	2,934,000	9.4	1,639,000	55.9
1895	2,120,000	6.7	1,256,000	59.3
1897	2,121,000	6.6	1,242,000	58.5
1900	2,249,000	6.9	1,310,000	58.3
1904	2,541,000	7.5	1,594,000	62.7
1909	1,293,000	8.3	1,904,000	65.0
1913	8,443,000	23.2	5,101,000	60.4
1919	10,239,000	27.3	5,794,000	56.6
1921	11,477,000	28.7	6,701,000	58.4
1924	11,939,000	29.0	7,614,000	63.8
1946	28,005,000	61.7	24,947,000	89.1

Source: F. Levi, U. Levra, N. Tranfaglia (eds) *Storia d'Italia I* (Florence: La Nuova Italia, 1978), p. 260.

These rounded figures show Italy's slow road to political democracy. Note the dramatic effect of electoral reform in 1882, 1912 and 1946 on the numbers of people with the right to vote. But note also the relatively low levels of political participation (those who actually voted).

universal mission of looking after the interests of Catholics everywhere. Pope Pius XI thought that the new Italian state had illegally taken away the Church's rights, and in 1874 he instructed Italian Catholics not to vote nor stand in elections to the national parliament. Effectively, the Church refused to recognise that the new state was legitimate and prevented Catholics from participating in political affairs at the national level. The situation was eased in the years just before the outbreak of the First World War, but it is difficult to underestimate the seriousness of the Church's exclusion of Catholics from national politics. It was no wonder that the first aims of the educational reforms in Italy were to get rid of the Catholic schools and teachers in the public sector and introduce secular teachers and teaching in state schools, something which, in practice, took some time to achieve.

Participation in Politics

With instruction in civic behaviour on the school curriculum, it was intended that even a basic primary education would equip young Italians to be future citizens of the national state. In Italy, it was literally the case that education qualified men for political participation. Literacy, being able to read and write, was retained as the requirement for adult males to vote in parliamentary elections, when electoral reform in 1882 increased the electorate from about 600,000, just over two per cent of the total population, to about two million men, just under seven per cent of the population. These figures indicate just how narrow the political base of the new Italy was, and just how low educational levels were. Catholic abstention from national elections helped to lower the numbers of men who actually voted to, perhaps, a half of the electorate. Again in Italy, as in other European national states, democratic politics and the exercise of citizens' rights and duties were regarded as part of the process of making the nation. Voting in national elections would, apparently, encourage men to take a national rather than local perspective or at least be aware of a world beyond the locality, especially when central government was beginning to provide services for ordinary people on a nationwide scale, such as schools, communications and welfare, which individuals could not supply from their own resources. A vote was some kind of say in the allocation of society's resources which were gathered in through national taxes by central government.

In reality, politics did not have these apparently 'nationalising' effects in Italy. Liberal nationalist politicians in Piedmont had assumed that the backwardness of much of the rest of the country, especially the south and Sicily, was down to the lack of political change and the rule of reactionary and illiberal governments. They thought that the situation would be transformed once people became citizens rather than subjects and began to exercise their political and individual rights and benefit from equality before the law. This was an illusion from the start, because of the liberals' own awareness of the fragility of the nation and its political institutions. They did not want to allow people to exercise their political and personal rights when this could threaten the very survival of the liberal state. The franchise or right to vote was limited and qualified because extending the vote to illiterate Catholic peasants, who were told by the Pope through their priests to have nothing to do with the country's political affairs, was to deliver the liberal state into the hands of its enemies.

Liberal governments were always distrustful of what they saw as the uneducated, unenlightened and unpredictable 'masses'. Any liberal system of government had to balance individual freedom and social order, and the liberal governments of Italy tended to protect order at the expense of liberty. This was expressed in the telling phrase, 'prevention not repression', coined by Marco Minghetti, a right-wing liberal who, as Minister of the Interior, was in charge of the country's police forces in the 1860s and was Prime Minister between 1873 and 1876. In practical terms, this policy meant that the police were more likely to ban a march or a demonstration, or an organisation, in case it caused trouble, rather than allow the event to take place and intervene only if a disturbance actually occurred. This kind of preventive rather than repressive policing effectively discouraged individuals and groups from exercising their right to meet, associate and organise.

Liberal Governments

The workings of the country's parliamentary system are best understood in the light of the separation which grew up between 'legal' Italy, meaning parliament, the government and the state administration, and the 'real' Italy of the bulk of the people who were politically excluded both by the narrow franchise and the Pope's ban on Catholic political participation. Starting with the governments formed by a left liberal politician, Agostino Depretis, who was Prime Minister at various points between 1876 and 1887, coalition cabinets were put together through a process which became known as *trasformismo*. This is not an easy term to translate or explain. There were not really any political parties among liberals in either the constituencies or parliament, partly because the electorate was so small that candidates could manage elections without the need for the support of any permanent political organisation. Instead, liberal deputies joined loosely organised and regionally based parliamentary lobby groups and attached themselves to leading politicians likely to become ministers or heads of governments. The lack of well-defined party groupings among parliamentary deputies was both cause and effect of the practice of prime ministerial candidates co-opting apparent political rivals into government, offering them ministries and hence ensuring that their hangers-on would become part of the government's parliamentary majority. *Trasformismo* fudged political differences between liberal politicians, and seen in its best light, was the way in which they could co-operate in government against the 'real' Italy of clerical reaction and democratic and socialist movements which, from their perspective, threatened the survival of the State. *Trasformismo*, seen in its worst light, led to corrupt and personalised rather than issue-led parliamentary government, because what sustained it was the promise of ministerial office and the flow of patronage, favours and influence to parliamentary supporters of the government and their small educated, well-off and propertied electorates. Deputies representing the south and the islands did well out of the system, and provided the parliamentary majorities for successive governments. This had serious consequences for the formation of the nation, since the workings of *trasformismo* widened the already significant political and economic gap between northern and southern Italy. The southern deputies and their electorates of middle-class professionals and landed nobility lived off an unproductive system of agricultural landholding, where large mainly grain producing estates, called *latifundia*, were exploitatively managed by land agents in the absence of the owners and worked by an army of agricultural labourers, some of them landless, others owning or renting small plots of land at subsistence levels, barely

10

enough to live on. The southern deputies lent their votes in support of governments in parliament in return for governments not embarking on land reform in the south and hence not changing the existing socio-economic structures on which they were dependent. In effect, the backwardness of the south was an integral part of the operation of what passed as parliamentary politics in Italy.

The idea of *trasformismo* is an important one to grasp because many historians and political scientists think that it characterised the way politics worked in Italy from the late nineteenth century to recent times. Depretis applied what was essentially a tactic of compromise with and co-option of men in parliament who appeared to be his political opponents. But both the co-opters and the co-opted belonged to the same narrow political class governing the country, and *trasformismo* was a way of unifying the political class of 'legal' Italy against 'real' Italy and ensuring its continued exercise of political power. But the term developed a wider meaning and significance, taking in the relations between the governing class and the rest of society and describing the way the former attempted to accommodate, absorb or, more crudely, buy off different and conflicting political and social forces. This was evident in the 'transformist' strategy of the dominant political figure of the early 1900s, the liberal politician Giovanni Giolitti, who was Prime Minister of three relatively long-lasting governments between 1903 and 1914, significantly overlapping with and stimulating a rapid spurt of economic development.

The Economy

Italy had a mainly agricultural economy, even by 1915. Although most Italians were 'urban' and lived in small to medium-sized towns, their livelihoods came mainly from owning, working on or providing services for agricultural land. But changes had occurred from the mid-1890s. There was not only growth in Italy's traditional textile and food processing industries, connected to greater mechanisation and the development of new products and techniques like sugar refining and canning. A capital-intensive, heavy industrial economy of iron and steel, shipbuilding, metal-making, engineering, automobile and chemicals production began to emerge. This was facilitated by the interaction of a number of factors, including a worldwide expansion of trade and markets, the application of Alpine hydro-electric power to both public utilities and industry which partly made up for the lack of coal resources, the growth of powerful investment banks with political connections to governments, which both protected newly-emerging and otherwise uncompetitive industrial firms and stimulated demand by ordering military hardware and spending heavily on infrastructure, from railways to land reclamation. Agricultural production and productivity also improved, reacting to and on the growth of the chemical fertiliser and machine industries and benefiting from government-funded land reclamation schemes and state protection of domestic grain and sugar producers.

This period of rapid growth in both industry and agriculture at the turn of the century had two important aspects. The level of state involvement in economic development was high, and unhealthily close relations developed in major industrial and agricultural sectors such as iron and steel, shipbuilding and armaments, electricity generation, wheat and sugar, between the banks who invested in companies in return for shares in them, the government which provided the orders and protected the home market, and the protected and subsidised firms themselves, whose economic survival was reliant on political lobbying and contacts. Economic growth was concentrated in the north and centre, rather than the south of the country, worsening the imbalance between northern and southern Italy. Industry expanded in the northern regions of Lombardy, Piedmont and Liguria, with the cities of Milan, Turin and Genoa the points of Italy's 'industrial triangle'. The land reclamation projects on the Po Valley plains of Piedmont, Lombardy, Venetia and Emilia led to social transformation. Peasants renting or share-cropping small plots of land gave way to large profit-driven tenant farmers who ran their estates like factories, hiring and firing as necessary a vast army of now landless under-employed agricultural labourers. Class conflict was bitter and long lasting in these areas of capitalist farming, and the combative labourers' organisations were the most important arm of the Italian socialist movement. In contrast, the south and islands lagged behind economically, with mass emigration to other European countries and overseas to the Americas both the most evident sign of its unproductive, overpopulated and impoverished agricultural economy and the only way to improve the conditions of life of those who remained.

Giolitti

Giolitti's version of *trasformismo* aimed to neutralise the political and social effects of Italy's partial economic modernisation by playing off Catholics and socialists. The Catholic Church was still officially unreconciled to the existence of the Italian state, and although a Catholic political party had not been formed, the Church had a vast network of social, welfare, charitable and economic associations through which it continued to influence Italian society. Giolitti recognised the socially conservative weight of the Church and attempted to lever it into action against the Socialist party, which had organised from the early 1890s among northern industrial and agricultural workers. In local and then national political deals, Giolitti encouraged Catholics to vote for and with liberals in conservative electoral alliances against socialists, moves which effectively meant the abandonment in fact if not in principle, of the Pope's ban on Catholic political participation.

Like most other Marxist socialist parties in Europe, the Italian socialist party uneasily included both those who believed that the party should be revolutionary in both means and ends, and those who believed in evolutionary change to be achieved through reforms of the existing political and socio-economic system and co-operation with non-socialist democratic parties. Giolitti's *trasformismo* to the left aimed to strengthen the reformists at the expense of the revolutionaries in the Socialist party and eventually co-opt the reformists into his government, by conceding social reforms, mediating in labour disputes rather than using the police against workers and finally, in 1912, granting the vote to nearly all adult males. Such *trasformismo*, as before, depended on and perpetuated the north-south divide. Giolitti's social and political reforms were directed at the industrialising north in an attempt to win over new popular movements whose growth was related to economic development. His parliamentary majorities were still made up of deputies from the south, and there he kept to the usual methods of electoral interference and patronage, not wanting to change the social and economic patterns of life which sustained southern liberal politicians and their clienteles. Giolitti's *trasformismo* to the left was, ultimately, unsuccessful. The Socialist party came out in opposition to participation in government and to the war between Italy and Turkey in 1911-12, which gave Italy possession of Libya in North Africa, but allowed the revolutionary wing to take control of the Socialist party from the reformists.

3 Key Personalities

Italo Balbo (1896-1940)

Balbo was the stereotypical Fascist hero. A personally charming and elegant young man from a middle-class background, he actively supported Italy's intervention in the First World War and was decorated for bravery as a junior officer in the Alpine regiment. A natural organiser and leader, he was approached by farmers of the Po Valley province of Ferrara to head the local *fascio*, and reportedly replied, 'How much does it pay?' Reassured on this point, he organised the province's Fascists into military formations to smash workers' unions not only in Ferrara but throughout the region. He helped to set up the 'March on Rome' and became chief of the Fascist Militia. First junior minister and then full Minister of Aviation between 1926 and 1933, Balbo personally organised and participated in a double-crossing of the north Atlantic from Italy to Chicago by seaplanes, a feat which made him an international celebrity and associated Fascism with daring, adventure and excitement, if serving little practical purpose, other than making Mussolini jealous of a Fascist leader whose standing rivalled his own. On his return from Chicago, Mussolini pushed him off into a kind of political exile as Governor of Libya, which he attempted to transform into a model Italian colony. He was his own man, to the extent that he was openly contemptuous of the Lateran Pacts and of the corporative system, and disagreed with the Axis connection with Germany and the anti-Jewish measures. But, like most other Fascist leaders, he never broke with Mussolini and the Fascist regime, and the comfortable and powerful place he occupied in it. He was commander of the Italian armed forces in North Africa, and in June 1940 was shot down and killed by Italian anti-aircraft gunners who mistook his aircraft for the enemy, perhaps a fitting end to a very Fascist life.

Gabriele D'Annunzio (1863-1938)

Born in the Adriatic town of Pescara, D'Annunzio was a major literary figure by the early 1900s, famous or notorious for his scandalously pleasure-seeking life style, which matched his decadent, erotic novels and poetry glorifying the masculine will and the 'great man', and his extreme nationalist and imperialist views. In 1914-15 he was the star attraction of the rallies and demonstrations which were organised to get Italy into the war. Although well beyond the normal fighting age, he volunteered for combat and spent the war staging a series of spectacular individual dare-devil stunts, including a flight over the Austrian capital, Vienna, to drop propaganda leaflets. A bitter critic of the post-war liberal governments' failure to translate military victory into more territorial gains, he marched into the disputed city of Fiume in September 1919 at the head of a band of war veterans. He ruled there for just over a year as if the city was his personal theatre, staging public rituals and ceremonies which Mussolini later adopted to cultivate the myth of the *Duce*. Effectively sidelined after Fiume by Mussolini, who saw him as his most serious political rival, D'Annunzio retired to live in luxury in his villa on the Italian lakes, and was fêted by the Fascist regime as Italy's greatest living artist.

Giovanni Giolitti

The most important liberal politician of his age, the Piedmontese-born Giolitti was Prime Minister of three lengthy governments between 1903 and 1914. He masterminded a political strategy which combined the partial political and economic modernisation of the country with the continuation of the corrupt and clientelistic politics of the south, and earned him the derogatory name of 'minister of the criminal underworld'. He thought that Italy should remain neutral in the First World War, but did not oppose the war once Italy had entered it. Making his political comeback in 1919 with a programme of reforms around which he hoped to unify the liberal factions and continue the strategy interrupted by the war, he was Prime Minister for the last time in 1920-1 and the pivotal figure of early post-war politics. Attempting to 'transform' the Fascists in the same way as he had tried to 'transform' the Catholics and reformist socialists before 1914 he, like the rest of the liberal political establishment, seriously underestimated the subversive and violent dynamism of the Fascist movement, a misjudgment which made him willing to accept Mussolini in power and even to approve the 1923 Acerbo Law which allowed the Fascists to dominate the Italian parliament. He did not stand in the 1924 elections as a member of the Fascist list, however, and although not boycotting parliament after Matteotti's murder, he eventually came out in opposition to the Fascist government. He died in 1928, long enough to see the consequences of and regret his mistaken evaluation of Fascism.

Benito Mussolini (1883-1945)

The founder of Fascism and the dictator of Italy, Mussolini was born in Predappio, a small place in the Romagna region of central Italy, the son of a blacksmith and innkeeper, and a primary school teacher. He was by temperament a rebellious and difficult young man, scruffy, unconventional and anti-establishment, a loner who did not really like or get on with other people. He lived a rootless and disorganised existence in Italy, Switzerland and Trento, then part of the Austrian empire, working intermittently as a teacher and labourer, and getting involved in socialist politics as an agitator and

journalist. Finally settling back in his home province of Forlì, he was leader of the local socialists and a nationally-known spokesman of the revolutionary wing of the Socialist party, joining the party's ruling body and becoming editor of the party's national newspaper, *Avanti!* in 1912. True to his activist style of politics, Mussolini broke with the Socialist party's neutralist stance in the First World War in late 1914, founding his own newspaper, *Il Popolo d'Italia*, which promoted Italy's intervention in the war. An effective and spiky communicator in both print and speech, he remained the journalist throughout his Fascist political career, and carried over into politics the popular journalist's concern with instantaneous, day-to-day drama and sensation. A very shrewd and manipulative political operator over the short term, and able to extract maximum political advantage from most situations, he managed to lead the Fascist movement to power in 1922 by combining talk of compromise with the threat of a violent insurrection. A sense of mission and longer-term strategy to make Italy great became evident with the establishment of the 'totalitarian' state, and the conquest of Ethiopia in 1935-6. Although still basically an insecure and impressionable person, he almost came to believe his own political myth as the *Duce*, the infallible great leader of his country, and his distrust of other people and excessive faith in his own political genius, increasingly isolated him in government. Characteristically, he blamed Italy's disastrous military performance in the Second World War on the inadequacies of his raw material, the Italian people who, according to him, behaved like sheep, not wolves, in war, the only form of activity that mattered for Fascists.

Victor Emmanuel III (1869-1947)

Victor Emmanuel was King of Italy from 1900 until his abdication in 1946. A cautious, timid and taciturn person, who rarely said anything in public or in private about the politicians whom he nominated as Prime Minister, he kept strictly to his constitutional role as monarch and often used this as a cover for his lack of political initiative and inaction. He took a more active role in foreign policy and military affairs, as constitutional practice allowed, and backed the Salandra government's efforts to get Italy into the war in 1914-15. As the nominal commander-in-chief of the armed forces, he spent the war away from Rome at the front. His inaction in October 1922, at the time of the

'March on Rome', and in the summer of 1924, during the Matteotti crisis, directly favoured Mussolini and Fascism. He went along with the establishment of the 'totalitarian' state, which seriously undermined, if did not abolish, his powers, and with the Nazi alliance and anti-Jewish laws, and agreed to declare war on France in 1940. He seemed to be pessimistically aware that his throne was under threat whether Fascism won or lost the war. But when the war went badly, he took an age to agree to the dismissal of Mussolini, which followed the Grand Council meeting of July 1943, but was firm in his preference for a government of civil servants which would not include any anti-Fascist politicians. After the armistice in September 1943, he fled to the south and Allied protection, leaving Rome undefended and no clear orders to the armed forces. With the continuation of the monarchy now very much dependent on the Allies, he reluctantly gave way to his son in May 1946. But, partly because of his long-term association with Mussolini's dictatorship, the monarchy was abolished in a referendum while Victor Emmanuel himself was in exile in Egypt.

4 Italy in the First World War

By 1915, the character of the First World War changed as a result of the lack of a speedy and decisive victory for either side. It was to be a long haul, and continuing to fight the war now depended on governments effectively mobilising all the country's human and material resources. The transition to what was called 'total war' came from the realisation that the 'fighting front' was reliant on the organisation and collective effort of the 'home front'. The need to wage a 'total war' posed similar kinds of challenges to all belligerent countries, and led to broadly similar responses which involved, above all, governments assuming control of the organisation of national economies for war. Securing the 'home front' also required governments to create and maintain some sort of balance between different political, social and interest groups, ensuring at least a kind of equality of sacrifice, in order to unite everybody behind the war effort. Governments had to guarantee a wartime political, social and economic truce, and get people to suspend the individual and collective disputes and conflicts of peacetime life. This was a difficult thing to achieve, because the organisation of a war economy was actually divisive. Certain activities had to be given priority over others: the channelling of resources to industries servicing the war effort was at the expense of the production of consumer goods, which became scarce and expensive, and this basic choice affected employment, labour mobility, and wage, price and profit levels throughout the economy. In this light, the ordeal of 'total war' was the test of the country's governmental and socio-economic systems and of its national cohesion.

The Russian Revolutions of 1917 can partly be explained by the political, social and economic strains set up by wartime mobilisation and government's inability to manage the wartime economy efficiently and fairly, to the point that its very legitimacy was challenged. In Italy, the system did not collapse, and for the mainly peasant conscripts in the Italian army, Italy's involvement in the First World War was their first great national experience. But the war did not produce even a temporary national unity, and the divisions widened by the wartime experience made people feel even less attached to the liberal parliamentary state while raising their expectations of changing it.

Italy Joins the War

Italians and their political leaders did not even agree on entry into the war. Italy was linked to Austria-Hungary and Germany in the Triple Alliance, but

Document 4   The Italian Prime Minister, Salandra, decides on war against Austria, in a conversation with the Minister of Colonies, Ferdinando Martini, September 1914.

'We cannot hesitate: if I were to think that I had the chance of restoring Trento and Trieste to Italy and I let it slip, then I would have no more peace of mind and I should ask myself what on earth I spent thirty years in parliament for.'

Source: C.J. Lowe and F. Marzari, *Italian Foreign Policy, 1870-1940* (London: Routledge, 1975), p. 390.

in May 1915 joined the war on the side of Britain and France once the right-wing liberal Prime Minister, Antonio Salandra, had negotiated a secret treaty promising Italy additional territorial gains in south-eastern Europe. There was no prior consultation of parliament, where a majority of Giolitti's liberals, and Catholic and socialist deputies, wanted Italy to remain neutral and not participate in the war. The neutralist majority were the targets of the street demonstrations and press campaigns of the 'interventionists', a strange coalition whose common ground was the desire to get Italy into the war. This cause brought together men from the democratic left, Nationalists, and groups of revolutionary syndicalists, Socialists and ex-socialists, including Mussolini, who broke with the Italian Socialist party because, unlike most of the other European socialist parties, it opposed the war. The revolutionary syndicalists believed that socialism was to be achieved by workers taking economic action (strikes) and developing their economic organisations (trades unions), rather than organising themselves in a political party. Most of them broke away from the Socialist party in 1907. These 'interventionist' groups had different and incompatible war aims, but they all saw the war as the opportunity to bring about radical political change in Italy.

The War in Italy

If the country was divided over Italy joining the war, then the prolongation of the war made things worse, as the government struggled to achieve the internal social truce for an efficient organisation of the war effort. The Italian Socialist party, uniquely in Europe outside Russia, was officially committed to peace and neutrality throughout the war. This stance encouraged the government and employers to impose harsh controls on industrial workers in factories. Money wages rose for workers in the war-related industries, but food supplies became scarce and more expensive in the industrial cities of the north, provoking food riots in Turin in 1917 where workers expressed their opposition to the war. In this atmosphere, the military defeat at Caporetto in late 1917 had dramatic internal repercussions. The disaster was blamed on national disunity, on the 'subversion' of the war effort by defeatist and pacifist forces, and led the government to put greater controls over the labour movement and the Socialist party. Government repression reinforced the revolutionary outlook of the Socialist party, as did the example of the Bolshevik

Revolution in Russia in October 1917, which seemed to indicate that war would lead to violent overthrow of the capitalist state.

The need after Caporetto to rally the country behind what was now a war to liberate Italian territory from occupying Austrian and German armies, induced the government to popularise the war by promising a better world to those fighting it. Most governments of belligerent countries did the same in the last year of the war, in order to combat popular war weariness and the appeal to workers of the revolutionary changes in Russia. The government's attempt to give a popular meaning to the war, portraying the post-war renewal of Italian society as the reward for the soldiers' service to the nation, contributed to that climate of a general expectation of wide-ranging change which was called '1919-ism'. Several post-war movements, including Fascism, attempted to exploit this mood for change generated by war mobilisation.

Mussolini and the War

The war certainly changed Mussolini, the founder of the Fascist movement. In 1914, he was a socialist organiser, journalist and propagandist, who had become an important leader of the Socialist party's revolutionary wing, and was editor of the party's national newspaper. His move from socialism to Fascism was, and is often seen as, simply the action of an unprincipled political opportunist. But his Socialist party position made him a national political figure, and the break with the party was a risk to his political career. What makes understandable Mussolini's political evolution from socialist to interventionist to Fascist was the rather unorthodox character of his socialism. He attempted to combine in his own thought and action the Marxist idea of class struggle with a half-digested reading of late nineteenth and early twentieth century writers, like Nietzsche, Sorel and Le Bon, who criticised the prevailing rational, determinist culture which politically found expression in liberalism and reformist rather than revolutionary socialism. This cocktail of ideas produced in Mussolini an elitist view of mass politics. In his view, the task of the Socialist party as a revolutionary elite was to use propaganda and direct action to tone up the workers for violent revolution. He believed that leaders did not have to wait on events, but could change and shape them by action and willpower, and that ideas and ideals had value to the extent that they were capable of arousing mass enthusiasm and commitment for revolutionary action.

From this perspective, the Socialist party's pacifist and neutralist position at the outbreak of war meant that an apparently revolutionary party did nothing, when for Mussolini a war of such scale and dimensions was really a revolutionary opportunity. Expelled from the party in late 1914, Mussolini campaigned for Italy's entry into the war through his own newspaper, funded by the French government and some Italian industrialists. This described itself as a 'socialist' newspaper until mid-1918, when it claimed to be the mouthpiece of 'combatants and producers'. The change of title indicated that Mussolini now wanted to represent and organise for political action a new 'revolutionary class' thrown up by the experience of war. He spoke of a 'trenchocracy', an heroic elite of worker-soldiers and peasant-soldiers who, by merit of their wartime struggle and sacrifice to save the nation, would reshape Italy on the lines of what he called 'an anti-Marxist and national socialism'.

This appeal to the war generation and the sense that the war experience had created the model of a new national society, rang true for many soldiers, not so much the peasant infantrymen as the young middle-class volunteer and conscripted junior army officers who experienced trench warfare alongside the men under their command. There was a very sharply felt physical and mental distance separating the 'home front', where the war hardly figured as a real threat to life, and the monotonous but murderous existence of soldiers in the trenches. This helped to create the feeling among frontline troops that they were a breed apart. They were often disgusted and disorientated while on leave by the normality of life behind the lines, and resented those 'sharks' and 'shirkers' who stayed behind in safety to exploit their patriotic sacrifice, the war profiteeers and industrial workers benefiting from the high prices and wages of the wartime economy. Instead, they found their sense of worth and belonging lay in the 'community' of the trenches. This experience was idealised by war veterans after the war, but it was how they lived and re-lived their war. It is impossible to understand the appeal of Fascism to these young men without grasping the meaning they gave to fighting in the war. Augusto Turati, a journalist of sorts before the war, an interventionist and volunteer who was decorated for bravery as an infantry officer and joined the Fascist movement after the war, becoming national head of the Fascist party in the late 1920s, wrote to a friend from the front that the 'real' Italy and Italians were not in 'civilian' Italy, but here in the trenches, and the 'idea' for which they were fighting was that 'Italy must be great, free, strong'.

Questions to Consider

- What were Italy's war aims?
- Did the First World War contribute toward Italian unity or disunity?
- Did the First World War create Italian Fascism?

5 Italy 1918-22

The 1919 election in Italy was the first real democratic vote in the country since unification in 1870. Every adult male had the vote, and a proportional representation system was introduced. Two parties, the Socialist party and a new Catholic party called the Italian Popular party, benefited most from the coming of mass political democracy and from '1919-ism', that general popular mood for change aroused by the wartime experience and the Russian revolutions of 1917. The socialists won 156 seats and the Catholic party 100 seats in the new parliament, while the liberals had 220 seats. This balance between the parties remained basically the same after the election of 1921. So, for the first time ever, parliament connected to the nation; parties with mass popular support were represented in parliament in proportion to their actual strength in the country.

Political Instability

In this case, as with most proportional representation systems, a government had to be formed by a coalition among the parties and groups with seats in parliament. It proved, however, difficult to achieve stable coalition governments in the period 1919-22, for several reasons. Liberals could not form a government with a parliamentary majority on their own, and anyway

Scene from the Russian revolution, an event which contributed to the 1918-ism popular mood

Documents 5a. The Russian Bolshevik leader, Lenin, encourages Italian Socialist party leaders to extend revolution from Russia to Western Europe, in a letter of December 1918.

'Dear Comrade Serrati!
My best wishes to you. We all hope that in Italy and in the other countries of the Entente a proletarian revolution will soon start...
Ever yours,
Lenin.'

Source: G. Bonfanti, *Il fascismo 1 La conquista del potere* (Brescia: La Scuola, 1976), p. 47.

5b. The Catholic version of a democratic Italy in an extract from the programme of the Catholic party, the PPI, early 1919.

'For a centralising state wanting to limit and regulate every organic power and every civic and individual activity, we wish on the constitutional plane to substitute a truly popular state that recognises the limits to its activity, that respects the natural units of the family, classes and the locality, that respects the individual personality and encourages private activity. And in order for the state to express the popular will, we want parliament to be reformed on the basis of proportional representation and of votes for women, and an elected senate which directly represents national, academic, administrative and union bodies; we want reform of the bureaucracy and the judiciary ... the recognition of local autonomy ... and the greatest possible decentralisation to regions.'

Source: G. Bonfanti, *Il fascismo 1 La conquista del potere* (Brescia: La Scuola, 1976), pp. 53-4.

5c. The election platform of the Socialist party in the north Italian city of Brescia, in the local elections of autumn 1920. The socialist gains in these elections made many middle-class people afraid that a series of local revolutionary socialist republics would be set up.

'With the conquest of the local municipal administrations the socialists intend to bring about the dictatorship of the workers (intellectual and manual) through applying the formula "all power to the workers' council".
    'The workers' council (soviet) is the body by means of which proletarian power replaces the parliamentary system ...
    'The socialists will use its power in the municipality exclusively to look after the class interests of the entire proletariat ...'

Source: G. Bonfanti, *Il fascismo 1 La conquista del potere* (Brescia: La Scuola, 1976), p. 74.

---

did not operate as a unified party, failing to adapt to the demands of political democracy and retaining the loose and changeable formations based on region and personality which had worked in pre-war parliaments when the electorate was smaller. The largest single party in parliament was the Socialist party, and it should have been a leading partner in government under normal conditions. But conditions were not normal. The Socialist party still had a reformist, social democratic wing, but the party as a whole

Modern Italy

Italian general election results, 1919 and 1921:

	1919	1921
PSI (Socialist party)	156	139
		(includes 15 Communists)
PPI (Catholic party)	100	108
Liberals and allies	220	239
		(includes 36 Fascists)

Source: P. Morgan, *Italian Fascism, 1919-1945* (London: Macmillan 1995), p. 16.

These figures show the number of seats won in the chamber of deputies of the Italian parliament. It is a recipe for parliamentary paralysis: the liberals, disunited anyway, cannot govern alone, while the revolutionary PSI refuses to govern. Note the small number of Fascist deputies, and yet Mussolini was appointed Prime Minister in 1922.

was formally committed to bringing about socialist revolution on the back of the collapse of the bourgeois parliamentary state. As a revolutionary party, it refused to co-operate with other non-socialist groups and parties so as to make parliamentary government work. In its view, worse was better: government instability was to be actively promoted, because it would accelerate the revolutionary overthrow of state institutions. The Socialist party's refusal to participate in a political system it wanted to destroy, meant that liberals and the new Catholic party had to work together. The Pope had withdrawn the ban on Catholics participating in national elections in 1918, and the formation of the Popular party, led by a Sicilian priest, Luigi Sturzo, as a Catholic democratic alternative to liberalism and socialism, signified the full involvement of Catholics in the political life of the country, another very important bridging of the gulf between 'real' and 'legal' Italy. Catholic politicians did join coalition governments led by liberals, but a lasting political relationship was hard to build up. Important issues divided them. Many liberals were anti-clerical, opposed to the Church's influence in Italian society. They distrusted a party of Catholics apparently attached to a church which was against the very existence of the liberal nation-state, and would not allow liberal ministers to make concessions on agrarian reform, votes for women, and Catholic schools as the price for continuing Popular party support in parliament. Government crises were often prolonged by the difficulty of liberal and Catholic politicians finding enough common ground to form a government, and this uncertainty undermined the credibility and effectiveness of parliamentary government and helped to ease Fascism's entry to government in 1922.

The *biennio rosso*

More important for the operation and survival of Italy's new system of parliamentary democracy was the impact of the country's post-war crisis of

1919-20, called the *biennio rosso* or 'red two years'. This was a period of almost continuous political and social unrest in both the urban and rural areas of the country, lasting from the spring of 1919 until late 1920. The popular grievances and discontents of these months were not channelled or met in parliament. It was doubtful that they could have been, in the light of the socialists' non-participation and the chronic instability of the relations between liberals and Catholics. The post-war popular agitation was confronted outside parliament, and in a way which worked against parliamentary government.

The unrest of 1919-20 coincided with and, to some degree, was caused by a post-war economic crisis, as the country emerged from fighting a long and expensive war. The government had borrowed heavily from its own citizens and from Italy's richer allies and printed money in order to fund wartime economic mobilisation. The outcome was inflation, which continued into the post-war period. It cut away at the income of those who lived on renting out property, who had savings and lent money to the government, and hit all consumers. The popular agitation of the 'red two years' took the form of land occupations in the south, with peasant soldiers recently demobilised from the army returning home to claim the land they had been promised by the government in the war. In the countryside of the north and centre, it took the form of strikes by socialist and Catholic-led agricultural labourer and peasant organisations for better wages and tenancy agreements. In the northern industrial towns and cities, there were organised working-class strikes for improved pay and conditions.

The *biennio rosso* had two important aspects which made it appear to be no ordinary crisis. In the north and centre, the agitation of industrial and agricultural workers seemed to go beyond demands for better wages and conditions in order to meet the country's chronic wartime and post-war inflation. There were also calls for workers' control of factories and farms, which were a real challenge to the property ownership and management of agricultural and industrial employers. The climactic end of the *biennio rosso* in September 1920 was the sight of over half a million industrial workers occupying their factories and attempting to manage the plants and continue production on their own. To hard-pressed employers, it looked like the crisis of capitalism, the start of a socialist revolution. A farmer in the province of Bologna, at the heart of central Italy's capitalist agriculture, complained in 1920 that 'there are times when I don't know whether I'm in Russia or in Italy'. What made matters worse for these employers was that the government and the organs of the State were seen as unable or unwilling to protect property and order against a social revolution. This was especially the case in the more economically developed north and centre of the country, where the local state officials tried to mediate in rather than repress workers' disputes and the police were sometimes simply overwhelmed by the scale and duration of popular action. In the south, where socialist organisations were generally weak or non-existent, land occupations were led by Catholic or, more usually, war veterans' associations, and here peasant agitation was eventually contained by the police and landowners.

In a situation where the State appeared to be failing to keep order and protect property, the *biennio rosso* was Fascism's great political opportunity. It was from late 1920, at the very peak of labour unrest in both town and country, that Fascism became a mass movement, riding on a middle-class and patriotic reaction to what was perceived at the time as an actual socialist revolution taking place. The Fascist movement grew, above all, in the towns and countryside of northern and central Italy, and was largely absent in the south. By the time the movement became the Fascist party, in late 1921, it had probably about 300,000 members.

Questions to Consider

- Why was Italy so divided in 1919?
- What was the effect of '1919-ism' on Italy?
- What part did *biennio rosso* play in the rise of the Fascists?

6 Mussolini and the Fascist Movement, 1919-22

The first *fasci di combattimento*, which means combat or fighting groups, were formed in Milan and other northern towns and cities in 1919. They deliberately tried to maintain the wartime spirit in the immediate post-war climate of '1919-ism'. Their programme was a rather odd mixture of nationalism, anti-socialism and democratic, social and economic reforms, an attempt to give some content to the 'national socialism' that the new movement's leader, Mussolini, had written about in 1918. It was designed to attract the ex-servicemen, the 'trenchocracy', the new 'class' which Mussolini believed had been formed during, and as a result of, Italy's wartime experience. The *fasci* were seen as a 'movement' and not a 'party', to give the impression that they were a national organisation open to men of all social classes and political views, just as the army during the war had been a body of soldiers from different backgrounds united in fighting for the common cause of the nation. Mussolini liked to say that the programme of the *fasci di combattimento* was in the name. They were combat groups which would get things done and resolve problems through decisive action, taking steps to do what was necessary without worrying too much about justifying them. Fascism's no-nonsense and activist approach was again related to the way soldiers were held to behave when fighting in the war, and was expressed in the belief that violence was the most effective and final way of settling political arguments.

However, the *fasci* attracted only a minority of the generation who had fought and lived through the war. In 1919-20, they were a relatively unimportant movement, made up of the small number of ex-socialists and revolutionary syndicalists who, like Mussolini himself, had supported Italy's intervention in the First World War, some ex-servicemen, mainly junior rank officers, some university and secondary school students and some middle-class professional men and intellectuals. The movement's political isolation even among the majority of war veterans was confirmed in the poor showing of Mussolini's Fascist list of candidates in the 1919 elections, winning only 5,000 votes of the 270,000 cast in the city of Milan.

The 'Mutilated Victory'

Nationalist and imperialist from the start, the movement tried to gain political advantage from Italy's disastrous international situation. As a result of victory in the war, Italy had gained territory in the north-east from the old Austrian empire, bringing the country up to its natural physical Alpine

Document 6a. The opportunism and activism of the new Fascist movement and its hope of winning over the 'war generation' are conveyed in this extract from Mussolini's speech to the first meeting of the Milan fascio in March 1919.

'I have the impression that the present regime in Italy has failed. It is clear to everyone that a crisis now exists. During the war all of us sensed the inadequacy of the government; today we know that our victory was due solely to the virtues of the Italian people, not to the intelligence and ability of its leaders.

'We must not be fainthearted, now that the future nature of the political system is to be determined. We must act fast. If the present regime is going to be superseded, we must be ready to take its place. For this reason, we are establishing the fasci as organs of creativity and agitation that will be ready to rush into the piazzas and cry out, "The right to the political succession belongs to us, because we are the ones who pushed the country into war and led it to victory!"'

Source: C.F. Delzell (ed), *Mediterranean Fascism, 1919-1945. Selected Documents* (London: Macmillan, 1971), p. 10.

---

frontiers but including many German-speaking people as a consequence. But at the Versailles Peace Conference in 1919 the liberal government, led by Vittorio Emanuele Orlando and Salandra, demanded areas now part of the new state of Yugoslavia under the terms of the secret treaty which had brought Italy into the war on the side of Britain and France and, in addition, the Adriatic industrial port of Fiume. This had a mixed Italian and Croat population and was occupied by Italian troops at the end of the war. France and Britain had signed the secret treaty but did not support the claim to Fiume,

The Versailles Peace Conference, 1919, which led to the sense of a 'mutilated victory'

● **The 'Mutilated Victory'**

The social background of Fascist party members, 1921

	%
Farm workers	24.3
Urban workers	15.4
Seamen	1.0
Students	13.0
Private sector employees	9.8
Public sector (state) employees	4.8
Teachers	1.1
Members of professions (lawyers, doctors, etc)	6.6
Tradesmen and artisans	9.2
Industrialists (big and small)	2.8
Farmers and landowners (large, medium and small, including tenants)	12.0

Source: R. De Felice, 'Italian Fascism and the Middle Classes', in S.U. Larsen and others (eds) *Who Were the Fascists? Social Roots of European Fascism* (Bergen: Universitetsforlaget, 1980), p. 314.

The PNF has about 300,000 members at this time. It is on the basis of figures like these that Fascism claims to be a national movement, including people from all social classes. But many farm workers, because of the effects of squadrist violence in the countryside, are forced to join, and most of the members come from the north and centre of Italy, not the south and the islands. Note the high proportion of students; young men like some of you are joining the Fascist movement!

while the United States opposed both meeting the terms of the treaty and the concession of Fiume. The Italians withdrew from the conference as a protest, but could not change their allies' attitude over Fiume when they returned. This was the basis of the feeling in the country that Italy had won the war but lost the peace, that the victory was 'mutilated' by her allies and by the government's failure to defend Italy's national interests. When Orlando's successor as prime minister, Francesco Nitti, decided to withdraw Italian troops from Fiume, a group of war veterans and mutinous soldiers, aided by the Italian army on the border and led by the nationalist poet, Gabriele D'Annunzio, occupied the city in September 1919 to keep it 'Italian'. The coup was supported by the Fascist movement, and many members from the north-eastern *fasci* went off to Fiume to join D'Annunzio. He lorded it over the city until he and his followers were ejected by Giolitti in late 1920, introducing a corporative system of rule and a spectacular style of personal government which influenced the way Mussolini ran the country later. But D'Annunzio's activist style, his nationalism and his recruitment of war veterans made him too much of a rival to Fascism for Mussolini's comfort. Mussolini, much to the disgust of many Fascists, did not do anything to prevent or oppose the government's ending of the Fiume occupation and, by sitting on his hands, effectively undermined a serious political rival. By this

6b. Squadrism in action. Italo Balbo, the Fascist boss of Ferrara, bullies the police chief of a neighbouring province to provide him with the trucks he needs for 'punitive expeditions' across the region in the summer of 1922.

'I told the chief of police that I would burn down and destroy the houses of all socialists in Ravenna if he did not give me within half an hour the means required for transporting the Fascists elsewhere. It was a dramatic moment. I demanded a whole fleet of trucks ... My ostensible reason was that I wanted to get the exasperated Fascists out of the town; in reality, I was organizing a 'column of fire' ... to extend our reprisals throughout the province ... We went through ... all the towns and centres in the provinces of Forlì and Ravenna and destroyed and burnt all the Red buildings ... It was a terrible night. Our passage was marked by huge columns of fire and smoke.'

Source: C.F. Delzell (ed), *Mediterranean Fascism, 1922-1945. Selected Documents* (London: Macmillan, 1971), p. 37.

time, in late 1920, Mussolini realised there was more to be gained politically from involving the movement in the domestic issues raised during the *biennio rosso*.

The *squadristi*

From the summer of 1920, the *fasci* started to form armed and mobile para-military units or 'squads', and from the autumn they began to intervene in the bitter class conflict between employers and workers, especially in the large capitalist farms of central Italy. The squads were gangs of mainly middle-class young men, initially often students and ex-army officers with a taste for action and adventure and with the experience of organised violence from the war. Directly financed and equipped by farmers' and businessmen's associations, and spreading out from the provincial capitals into the sur-rounding small towns of the countryside, the squads literally took up the gun and the cudgel on behalf of employers and began a systematic campaign of violence to destroy workers' organisations. In so-called 'punitive expedi-tions', they ransacked and demolished socialist party and union premises, intimidated and beat up socialist organisers and leaders, organised and enforced tax boycotts against socialist-run local councils, sometimes forcing socialist councils to resign. The aim and effect of the campaign of violence was to take away the post-war political and economic gains of workers' organisations, and restore conditions of work favourable to employers. Intimidated agricultural workers were regimented into Fascist unions, or syndicates, with whom the employers 'negotiated' new wage rates and work-ing conditions which were worse than those won by the socialist unions they had replaced. Since farmers would only employ agricultural labourers who belonged to the syndicate, the *fascio* effectively controlled employment opportunities.

So, on the back of these violent squadrist offensives, Fascism won the

6c. The Fascist movement becomes the Fascist party in November 1921, and this extract from the PNF programme indicates something of the sense of the nation and the all-powerful state which was to inspire the setting up of the Fascist system of rule in the late 1920s.

'Fascism has now become a political party in order to tighten its discipline and clarify its "creed".

'…The nation is not simply a sum of human beings, nor is it an instrument for parties to attain their own goals. It is rather an organism made up of an endless series of generations whose individual members are but transient elements. It is the supreme synthesis of the material and spiritual values of the race.

'The State is the legal incarnation of the Nation …

'The autonomous values of the individual and those that are common to most individuals - expressed through such organised collective living entities as families, towns, corporations, etc - are to be promoted, developed and defended, but always within the context of the nation, to which they occupy a subordinate place.'

Source: C.F. Delzell (ed), *Mediterranean Fascism, 1919-1945. Selected Documents* (London: Macmillan, 1971), p. 28.

---

support of a broad coalition of middle-class people in town and country in northern and central Italy whose interests were threatened by the advance of working-class organisations and the fear of socialist revolution. By the summer of 1922, many provinces in these parts of the country were under a kind of informal military occupation of the Fascist squads, led by local Fascist party bosses who were called *ras* after the term for Ethiopian chieftains. These men had the real power in their provinces, and openly took over the authority and functions of government. They used the squads to terrorise their political opponents, creating such an intimidating climate that those whose official job it was to keep law and order, the police and magistrates, could not do so in an impartial way. The local Fascist party settled labour disputes and through the syndicates ran the labour market. The Fascist movement, which had taken off in 1920-1 as the violent reaction to what appeared to be the weakness of the state in the face of socialism was, in 1922, itself a threat to the State.

The Liberal Response

The subversive side of Fascism was not really recognised by the liberal politicians still running the government, who helped to bring about Fascism's coming to power at the centre in October 1922. Giolitti, who led a coalition government in 1920-1, tried to co-opt Fascism into the parliamentary system: Fascist candidates were elected to parliament in May 1921 as members of an electoral coalition put together by him. The intention was to tame Fascism by giving it a legal and parliamentary form and including it in what Giolitti hoped would be a coalition of conservative liberal interests. This attempt at *trasformismo* did not work. Giolitti welcomed the late 1921 transformation of the Fascist movement into a party, the National Fascist Party or *Partito Nazionale Fascista* (PNF), as a sign of its growing political respectability. But the change had been opposed by many *ras*, and the new party was not a normal one. It kept its character as a 'combat' organisation, an armed militia whose continual use of violence to settle things showed that it did not believe in dialogue or compromise with other political forces. The way the PNF behaved in areas it controlled, not tolerating any opposition to that control, was close to the kind of single party system of rule which Fascism finally became in the late 1920s, and made it completely out of step with democratic parliamentary politics which allowed differing viewpoints to be expressed and represented. While happy to exploit the willingness of liberal leaders like Giolitti to make a political deal with him, Mussolini well realised that his political influence came from his leadership of a movement whose power lay outside and against parliament in the paramilitary formations of squadrism. The effect of Giolitti's 'transformistic' inclusion of Fascists in his electoral coalition in 1921 was to strengthen Fascism, rather than contain it. The prefects, who were state officials with wide powers in the provinces including the police, were expected to use those powers at elections in favour of candidates on the sitting government's electoral slate. This now included the Fascists, and so it became difficult for prefects and police to take action against Fascist violence, even if they wanted to; tolerating, even aiding Fascist violence was now almost official policy. Giolitti's recruitment of Fascists to his electoral coalition also made Fascism more acceptable to local liberal leaders who were on the same slate. Both state authorities and local political leaders were, in effect, being encouraged to support Fascism in its anti-socialist crusade. Certainly, by the summer of 1922, when reformist socialists and Catholic Popular party leaders were considering the formation of an anti-Fascist coalition government which would take a stand against political violence, this proved impossible to achieve because many liberal and conservative Catholic politicians were convinced that the only way both to defeat Socialism and check Fascism was by giving Mussolini a share in power. The willingness of many liberal deputies to accept Mussolini as Prime Minister in October 1922 and support a period of emergency rule, brought parliament at the centre into line with the grouping of middle-class interests around Fascism in the provinces.

The 'March on Rome'

Fascism's coming to power in October 1922 was ambiguous, and was interpreted at the time and later by historians, in different ways. The Fascists planned and staged a coup, a violent seizure of power, which involved Fascist squads occupying government buildings in the provincial capitals of northern and central Italy, while three small squadrist armies moved towards the national capital in the so-called 'March on Rome'. The liberal government led by Luigi Facta had declared a state of emergency, and the army was called out to defend Rome. But the King, having agreed to martial law, then went back on his decision, which meant that the army would not now be used to resist the Fascists. Nobody really knows why the King withdrew the emergency law. But he was probably afraid that stopping the Fascists by force from coming to power would start a civil war, and this could be avoided if Mussolini was invited to lead a government, which was what many liberal leaders were recommending to him anyway. So Mussolini arrived from Milan to be nominated as Prime Minister by train, not at the head of his squadrist armies, which marched triumphantly through Rome the day after. The legal and constitutional forms were observed: the King had asked Mussolini to form a government in the normal way. But this was not a normal political crisis; the King and the liberal politicians he consulted were clearly giving in to the pressure of a violent Fascist movement. With only 36 seats in parliament, there was nothing in terms of parliamentary politics to show that the Fascists should head a government. Fascism was a problem because of its violent and illegal methods, which conservative liberal and Catholic politicians thought could be handled by including Fascism in government. Mussolini, meanwhile, with a private army at his disposal, could threaten an armed coup if he was not offered power in a constitutional and parliamentary way. He helped to plan a coup at the same time as he talked to liberal leaders about Fascists entering government, and the violent approach was probably a means of exerting pressure to bring about an apparently non-violent taking of power. The turn of events in October 1922 allowed liberals to play down the

The 'March on Rome'. Mussolini arrives in Rome in a taxi

revolutionary feel to the 'March on Rome'. The outcome was Mussolini heading a coalition government, which was approved by a majority in parliament; Mussolini and Fascism were 'in' the system. But for Fascists, the 'March on Rome' had a different meaning: it was a rising against the parliamentary system, the start of a Fascist 'revolution'.

Questions to Consider

- How important was the violence of the *squadristi* in the increasing   support for Mussolini?
- Was the PNF a political party in the period 1919-22?
- How influential was the Fiume incident in Mussolini's rise to power?
- Who was attracted to Fascism?
- Were the liberals naive to expect Mussolini to share power with them?
- Was the 'March on Rome' a revolution, or an orderly transfer of power?

7 Fascism in Power, 1922-5

When Mussolini became Prime Minister in October 1922, there had been no clean 'revolutionary' break with the existing political system and state institutions, such as occurred with the seizure of power by Lenin and the Bolsheviks in Russia in 1917. The King was still head of state, parliament was still operating, the civil service was still in place. The governments which Mussolini led between 1922 and 1925 were made up of Fascist, liberal and Catholic ministers, and up to the 1924 elections, depended on parliamentary majorities of non-Fascist groups and parties. The continued existence of the liberal state meant that people wondered for some time whether Mussolini would go on working in the liberal parliamentary system or make changes. It also meant that if change did occur, then it would happen gradually rather than quickly.

Which Way Forward?

There were all kinds of pressures on Mussolini from both inside and outside the Fascist party, some for making big changes, others for making limited changes. Those conservative liberal and Catholic politicians who backed Fascism in its campaign against the socialist threat wanted as little change as possible. They thought that Mussolini could provide a necessary but temporary period of strong government after the political chaos of the post-war years, which was why they voted in parliament to give the new government emergency powers for one year in economic, financial and administrative matters. They expected the PNF's violence to stop, now that the socialist enemy had been defeated.

The Fascists themselves were divided over what to do with the power they had won. A small but influential group also wanted the Fascist party to give up violence, unnecessary once Mussolini was head of the government, and deal in an organised way with making the State more efficient and well-run. This group was behind the setting up of special study units or 'think tanks' of experts whose job was to come up with proposals for the reform of the State and the services it provided. Another political group, the Nationalists, had a great influence on Mussolini's political thinking during the 1915-18 war and on the development of the Fascist regime in the mid to late 1920s. They merged with the PNF in 1923. While they had coherent plans for an authoritarian rather than a parliamentary system of government, they were monarchist and thought that change should come about through the orderly action

Document 7a. Mussolini's menacing first speech as Prime Minister to the Italian parliament in November 1922, which reveals the balance of violence and compromise which he used to come to power.

'For my part, I insist that the revolution has its rights ... I am here to defend and enforce in the highest degree the Blackshirts' revolution, and to inject it into the history of the nation as a force for development, progress, and equilibrium.

'I could have abused my victory, but I refused to do so. With 300,000 youths armed to the teeth, fully determined and almost mystically ready to act on any command of mine ... I could have transformed this drab, silent hall into a bivouac for my squads ... I could have barred the doors of parliament and formed a government exclusively of Fascists. I could have done so; but I chose not to, at least for the present ...

'I have formed a coalition government, not indeed with the object of obtaining a parliamentary majority - which I can get along very well without - but in order to rally to the support of this suffocating nation all those who, regardless of nuances of party, wish to save this nation.'

Source: C.F. Delzell (ed), *Mediterranean Fascism, 1919-1945. Selected Documents* (London: Macmillan, 1971) pp. 45-6.

---

of state organs rather than as a result of the PNF's violent and unpredictable conduct.

There were two other groups within Fascism who wanted to bring about radical change and who regarded the 'March on Rome' as the beginning of the end of parliamentary government. The syndicalists in the movement, many of whom had been with Mussolini from the interventionist campaign of 1914-15 and the start of Fascism in 1919, were certainly anti-socialist but did not see themselves as anti-worker. They wanted rather the 'nationalisation' of Italian workers, to attach them to the nation organised as a national syndicalist or corporate state. This meant that people would be organised and represented according to their economic functions, their role in the work place as 'producers'. The idea was that all 'producers' in the various sectors of the economy, whether they were manual workers, technical staff, managers and employers, would form or join together in mixed unions or 'corporations', which would not represent just one part of the work force which was the case with the existing class-based labour unions, but represent all the work force, everybody involved in the process of making things. Class conflict between workers and bosses which, through strikes and lockouts damaged production, would disappear as the various groups of 'producers' co-operated in the corporations and came to see that they had a common interest in increasing production and making it more efficient. Ideally, the 'producers' would organise their own affairs, but the Fascist idea of corporatism gave an important role to the State rather than self-regulation. State control was necessary to discipline what was still a divided society, and to impress on the corporations the priority of national production before

Italian general election results, 1924

	seats
National List	355
Other government lists	19
Total government supporters	374
Independent lists, initially supporting government	30
Opposition lists:	
PPI	40
Socialists and communists	65
Constitutional liberals	14
Republicans	7
Germans and Slavs	4
Independents	1
Total opposition	131
Total number of deputies	535

Source: C.S. Maier, *Recasting Bourgeois Europe. Stabilization in France, Germany and Italy in the Decade after the First World War* (Princeton: Princeton Uiversity Press, 1975), p. 438.

These elections, held under the Acerbo electoral law, where the list winning more than 25 per cent of the vote gets two-thirds of the seats in the chamber of deputies, give Mussolini an unchallengeable parliamentary majority. It effectively marks the end of parliamentary government in Italy.

individual or group interests. The natural allies of the syndicalists after 1922 were the squadrists and their leaders. They wanted to make permanent the control of provincial society won by the local Fascist party bosses in the 1920-2 period, and continue to use the same terroristic methods of control. Their idea of the Fascist 'revolution' was 'jobs for the boys', the replacement of the old political elites by the new hard men of Fascism, and the PNF controlling and taking over state bodies and functions, becoming the State.

A Creeping Dictatorship

The issues raised by these differing viewpoints on the direction Fascism should take now that it was in government were not really resolved until after 1925. What happened between 1922 and 1925 is difficult to interpret, but overall, what emerged was Mussolini's attempts to take over total power in a progressive and gradual way, a 'creeping dictatorship'. He created new Fascist party bodies which operated alongside and almost in competition with state and government bodies. The Fascist Grand Council was set up in December 1922, an assembly of the top Fascist leaders in PNF, state and syndicate posts. Although the Council was not an official or legal body until 1928, it only included Fascists and met to agree Fascist policy, working as a kind of separate Fascist cabinet to the actual cabinet of the coalition

Document 7b. In this government decree of January 1923, the Fascist squads become the Militia, a party army paid for out of public money. Notice that no other party is allowed to do the same.

'The Militia for National Security will serve God and the Italian fatherland, and will be under the orders of the Head of Government. With the help of the (police and army), it will be responsible for maintaining public order within the nation; and it will train and organise citizens for the defence of Italy's interests in the world …

'Expenses for the establishment and operation of the Militia…are to be charged to the budget of the Ministry of Interior.

'All parties whatsoever shall be forbidden to have formations of a military character after the present decree goes into effect …'

Source: C.F. Delzell (ed), *Mediterranean Fascism, 1919-1945. Selected Documents* (London: Macmillan, 1971), pp. 52-3.

---

government. It was the Grand Council which first decided to create the Fascist Militia or MVSN, which made the Fascist squads into a national para-military organisation funded by the taxpayer but at Mussolini's orders to keep internal order and give military training to the young people of Italy. The Militia was, in other words, a private army kept going at public expense, set up to keep Fascism in power, by force if necessary.

Despite the fact that Fascism was now in government, squadrist intimidation continued, both to maintain PNF control in those northern and central provinces where the *ras* were on top and also to extend that control into 'unfascistised' areas of the country. The provincial state officials, the prefects and the police, tolerated the continuing use of force by the dominant party against its political opponents, and used their own considerable local powers to the same end. This was especially important in supporting the steps being taken by the Fascist unions or syndicates to drive out rival Catholic and socialist unions and make sure that they and nobody else organised and represented workers in both agriculture and industry. On the pretext that they were badly run, prefects closed down unions, co-operatives and other workers' organisations, and their members, premises and assets passed to the Fascist syndicates. An agreement of December 1923 arranged by the government led to the industrial employers' organisation and the national Fascist organisation of workers' syndicates stating that they would co-operate with each other and keep out other organisations. This was hardly the mixed unions or corporations wanted by the Fascist syndicates. But it helped the Fascist syndicates, which were far weaker in industry than in agriculture, to claim a union monopoly and say that they were the only bodies allowed to represent industrial workers in negotiations with their employers.

Electoral Changes

The government also drastically changed the electoral system and, in so doing, practically undermined the basis of parliamentary democracy. The so-called Acerbo Law, which was passed by parliament in July 1923, said that the electoral slate which won the highest number of votes in an election, as long as this was more than a quarter of the total number of votes cast, would have two-thirds of the seats in parliament. This was a crude way of ensuring that the Fascist government had a guaranteed majority in parliament, and would do away with the need for Fascism to form a coalition government. The 1924 elections were held under the new system and delivered the expected results. The official government electoral slate won 65 per cent of the total vote and won 374 of the 535 seats in parliament. About two-thirds of the 374 deputies were Fascists. The rest were Nationalists, conservative liberals and Catholics and others, mainly from the south and the islands. This was really important, because these elections showed that Fascism had managed to split up and weaken the Catholic Popular party, one of its main political rivals before and after 1922. The Catholic party's conservative wing had left and joined the Fascist electoral list and been elected on a Fascist electoral ticket. This was Fascism's own version of *trasformismo*, the co-option of political opponents, and it was the way in which Fascism, originally strong in the north and centre but weak to non-existent in the south, entered southern politics. The southern liberal politicians and their local supporters were interested in contacts with the government in power, whatever its political line, in order to get their share of the State's resources. By getting them on to the 1924 governmental electoral list, which practically guaranteed election, the Fascist government 'transformed' these southern politicians into its supporters, repeating the tactics used by Giolitti in the south before 1915 and with the same effects.

The Matteotti Affair

So, the creation of PNF bodies parallel to and overlapping with state bodies, the PNF's continuing use of force to squeeze out rival organisations, the electoral reform which both made a nonsense of the parliamentary system and helped the government to weaken the Catholic party and spread its political hold over the south, together added up to a general move towards more authoritarian rule and the PNF monopolising political power. The pace of these changes was certainly speeded up as a result of Fascism's great crisis in 1924. When parliament met after the 1924 elections, a socialist deputy, Giacomo Matteotti, challenged the validity of the results, pointing to the PNF's violence and intimidation which, in some areas, had led to a 100 per cent vote for Fascist candidates. Matteotti was kidnapped and murdered in June by a gang of Fascists employed in a special unit of Mussolini's Press Office set up to harass political opponents. This was why the murder caused such a scandal: the Fascists held responsible were linked to and were, presumably, taking orders from people in government circles close to Mussolini himself. The opposition deputies withdrew from parliament in protest, and expected the King to dismiss Mussolini as Prime Minister of a government involved in criminal violence and nominate someone else to head a new and anti-Fascist government. But the King did not act, again probably because of the same fear of civil war which had led him to withdraw the emergency measures at the time of the 'March on Rome' in October 1922. Mussolini called up the Fascist Militia and had it armed by the army. If the government fell, here was the threat that the Fascists might well resist by force.

Mussolini ducked and dodged as best he could. He dismissed from their party and government posts the men implicated in Matteotti's killing, and agreed to the Militia becoming part of the regular army rather than a private army of the Fascist party. But in response to pressure coming from Fascists, he also agreed to the PNF proposal for the setting up of a Fascist state. Mussolini was, in other words, trying to satisfy both those who thought that the Matteotti crisis should lead to a more 'normal' government, where political violence had no place, and those in the PNF and Militia who wanted him to push ahead forcibly with the replacement of the parliamentary liberal state. Mussolini's balancing act could not last. In December, after an

The Matteotti affair was to haunt Mussolini. Here a British cartoonist alludes to it when Mussolini invaded France in 1940, suggesting that now many other Italians would die as Mussolini forces Italy onto French bayonets while the ghost of Matteotti looks on

● **The Matteotti Affair**

Document 7c. Mussolini in this famous speech to the chamber of deputies in January 1925, finally makes the break with the parliamentary system

'... I now declare before this assembly that I assume, I alone, full political, moral, and historical responsibility for all that has happened ... If Fascism has been nothing more than castor oil and the rubber truncheon, instead of being a proud passion of the best part of Italian youth, then I am to blame! If Fascism has been a criminal organisation, then I am the chief of this criminal association!

'... If all the violence has been the result of a particular historical, political, and moral climate, then let me take the responsibility for this, because I have created this historical, political, and moral climate with a propaganda that has gone forth from the intervention until today ...

'... You may be sure that within the next forty-eight hours after this speech, the situation will be clarified in every field.'

Source: C.F. Delzell (ed), *Mediterranean Fascism, 1919-1945. Selected Documents* (London: Macmillan, 1971), pp. 58-9.

---

opposition newspaper implicated Mussolini in the Matteotti murder, angry Militia officers, worried about the Militia reform and the survival of the Fascist government, confronted Mussolini and threatened that if he did not act against Fascism's opponents, they would do so without him. This dramatic intervention by hardline Fascists led to Mussolini making his notorious speech in parliament in January 1925 where he accepted responsibility for all that had happened and promised decisive action. So whatever uncertainty still remained about Fascism's position after 1922 finally disappeared as the result of the Matteotti crisis, which led Mussolini to make the decisive break with the liberal parliamentary system and set up the first ever 'totalitarian' state.

Questions to Consider

- Which options were open to Mussolini at the end of 1922?
- How far had Mussolini consolidated his power by 1925?
- Was Mussolini a dictator by the end of 1925?
- In what ways did the murder of Matteotti change Italian politics?

8 The Fascist State, 1925-40

The action promised by Mussolini took the form of various laws and decrees in 1925 and 1926 which effectively created a very repressive one-party police state. All parties and organisations opposed to the Fascist government were banned; the opposition deputies who had boycotted parliament after Matteotti's murder lost their seats; the opposition press was suspended and the rest was controlled; the death penalty was reintroduced for crimes against the State, and a Special Tribunal was set up to judge political crimes; the prefects, police and judges were given very wide powers over individuals, whom they could punish merely on the suspicion that they might do something wrong; elected local councils were abolished, and replaced by government-appointed officials. By late 1926, the Italian people had been deprived of their democratic rights and liberties to meet, speak and organise freely; it was now illegal to oppose the Fascist government in any way.

There were also changes to the way the country was governed. The law of December 1925 created a new position in place of the Prime Minister, called the Head of Government. As Head of Government, Mussolini was responsible for his actions only to the King not to parliament. He decided what business came before parliament, and could make laws by issuing a personal decree. This was the end of Italy's parliamentary system, since Mussolini had both legislative and executive powers. The same person made the laws and put them into effect, and was not accountable to a popularly elected parliament for his position as leader of the government or for his policy in government. A law of May 1928 downgraded parliament even more. People now simply voted 'yes' or 'no' to one huge list of candidates who were chosen by the Grand Council. Later in 1928, the Grand Council itself was made an official body, and as before was to decide on all major matters of government and PNF policy, and controlled the PNF. It was also meant to choose and update a kind of 'waiting list' of Fascists who would fill government posts when they became vacant and succeed Mussolini as Head of Government. In this way, the Grand Council could ensure that a Fascist government would carry on even when Mussolini died. It was as a result of these changes that the Fascist dictatorship came into being.

The Totalitarian State

But what made the Fascist system of rule different was its claim to be 'totalitarian', a term which was being used and applied to a political system for the

Document 8a. The police state in action, in an extract from the Public Security laws of 1931. Notice that the 'official warning' can be given to people who have not actually done anything, and the extent to which their freedom of movement can be restricted by the police.

'The chief of police can propose that the prefect issues a formal warning to unemployed idlers … and the people whom the public mark out as being dangerous to society or to the political order of the State …

'… The warning lasts for two years and is imposed by a provincial commission … called and chaired by the prefect …

'… The commission can require the person receiving the warning not to associate with convicted or otherwise suspicious people, not to return home late at night nor leave home in the morning before a specified hour, not to carry arms, not habitually to spend time in restaurants, pubs or brothels, and not to take part in public meetings.'

Source: A. Aquarone, *L'Organizzazione dello stato totalitario* (Turin: Einaudi, 1965), pp. 555-7.

---

first time anywhere. The most well-known definition of 'totalitarian' was the one provided by Mussolini: 'everything in the State, nothing outside the State, nothing against the State'. Mussolini's definition owed a lot to the ex-Nationalist lawyer, Alfredo Rocco, who was appointed Minister of Justice in January 1925 and produced most of the major laws which, between 1925 and 1928, established the Fascist state. Rocco's idea was that all organised groups in society should become legal organs of the State and under state control, in order to ensure that they controlled their members in a way which put the national interest first. So the 1926 syndical law said that only organisations recognised by the State could negotiate labour agreements on wages and working conditions which then had to be applied throughout the sector of the economy concerned. In industry, this meant that the Fascist industrial unions or syndicates gained the monopoly they wanted; they were the only organisations legally allowed to represent industrial workers. *Confindustria*, the industrial employers' association, became the sole body which legally spoke for employers.

The supremacy of state authority was also applied to the Fascist party. Up to the mid-1920s, the PNF had competed with, replaced or controlled state officials and bodies in many northern and central Italian provinces. Under the leadership of Roberto Farinacci, the *ras* of the northern province of Cremona, the PNF saw itself after Mussolini's January 1925 speech as the real 'totalitarian' body, extending its control over the activities of all organisations. But in the late 1920s, the PNF was itself reorganised. It was put under centralised control and discipline; the local party bosses who behaved like little dictators in their provinces were removed; and the state official, the prefect, was formally made the most important and powerful authority in provincial life, to whom the party leader was subordinate. As the subordinate instrument of

Agricultural and industrial production as a proportion of total national economic production (%)

	Sector	1913	1925	1938
Italy	agriculture	37	33	27
	industry	25	30	31
Czechoslovakia	agriculture	27	25	24
	industry	31	33	35
Germany	agriculture	23	16	15
	industry	45	56	58
Britain	agriculture	6	4	4
	industry	38	37	37
Hungary	agriculture	44	33	31
	industry	24	28	32
Switzerland	agriculture	23	17	12
	industry	35	38	42

Source: G. Toniolo, *L'economia dell'Italia fascista* (Bari: Laterza, 1980), p. 15.

A comparative look at Italy's move towards an industrial economy. Industry overtakes agriculture at the point when the Fascist government is still committed to the 'ruralisation' campaign.

the Fascist state, the PNF still had a very important 'totalitarian' role to play in the 1930s, but it was no longer really in a position to determine the Fascist government's policies.

The 'Battles' for Grain and the *Lira*

Like other governments in the 1920s and 1930s, the Fascist government had to deal with many economic difficulties and the so-called Great Depression of 1929-33, a worldwide economic crisis which was so severe in its effects on trade, production and employment, that people at the time thought the capitalist system itself was at the point of collapse. Some of the economic measures taken by the Fascist government were similar to those taken in other countries. But many were distinctively 'Fascist' policies, or policies which had a 'Fascist' approach or tone to them. Italy's economic problems in the late 1920s arose essentially because the country's economy was still comparatively weak in international terms. The strongest countries economically and financially were the United States and Britain, which decided to strengthen the value of their respective currencies, the dollar and the pound sterling. This revaluation of the major currencies in use in world trade and investment had the effect of lowering the value of, or devaluing, other currencies, including the Italian currency, the *lira*. This change in the values of currencies meant that Italy had to pay more than before for the imported goods it bought from other countries. So in 1925-6 the country was importing larger amounts of grain because of poor harvests and having to pay higher prices for it, which in turn pushed up prices, causing inflation, in Italy. In response, Mussolini decided to increase Italy's grain production by protecting Italian farmers against cheaper foreign imports, and to stop the fall in the value of the *lira*, promising publicly in August 1926 that the *lira*, at the time worth 150 to the pound, would increase in value to 90 to the pound.

There was nothing new in measures to protect Italian agriculture and the Italian currency. The difference was in the way Mussolini tried to mobilise the country behind what he called 'battles' for grain and the *lira*. Using terms of struggle, conflict and war was deliberate. Mussolini wanted to remind Italians of the spirit of wartime sacrifice, discipline and bravery and call these virtues into action again to make Italy economically stronger and independent of other nations. The aim of the 'battle for grain' was for Italy to produce all her own basic food resources and not be dependent on imported grain in order to feed the population, especially important if the country was to fight and survive a war. The goal was actually achieved by the late 1930s at the expense of the development of other areas of agriculture. Applied to the whole economy, the policy of economic independence and self-sufficiency was called 'autarchy'. This became the official policy of Fascism in the mid-1930s, when the government took action to prepare the Italian economy for war. A war was not being planned for in the late 1920s. But Mussolini's language and behaviour during the revaluation of the *lira* in 1926-7 displayed the warlike tone and appeal he gave to all his policies, and showed that he wanted to move the economy towards 'autarchy' from the start of the existence of the 'totalitarian' state.

'Ruralisation'

The 'battle for grain' became part of another larger campaign which was launched by Mussolini in 1927 and lasted throughout the Fascist period. This was to 'ruralise' Italy, make the country more 'rural'. Historians are rather puzzled by the 'ruralisation' campaign, because strengthening the agricultural sector of the economy seems an odd way of making the country stronger when, in the modern world, economic and military power comes from building up industry. For Mussolini, the strength of the nation came from a large and growing population capable of supplying Italy with the soldiers and settlers it needed to conquer and run an overseas empire. The real problem was Italy's declining birth rate, something which was affecting other European countries and causing their governments similar concern. The fall in births was greatest in industrial towns and cities, and so to reverse the trend people had to be encouraged to have more children, be prevented from moving from the countryside to the towns and a prosperous agriculture of child-producing peasants promoted. So, starting in 1927-8, the government tried to get people to marry earlier and have lots of children. Bachelors paid a special tax, whose proceeds went to improve the care of mothers and their children. The prefects and police were told to stop people moving to the cities and return to the countryside those who made the move. To make life in the countryside more appealing, the government spent huge sums of money on reclaiming and

Document 8b. The corporation in theory, if not in practice, in the report on the 1934 bill setting up the corporations by Alfredo Rocco, the ex-Nationalist who, as Minister of Justice, drafted the most important laws of the Fascist state.

'The key body in this new Fascist economy is the corporation in which the various categories of producers, employers and workers are all represented and which is certainly the best fitted to regulate production, not in the interest of any one producer but in order to achieve the highest output, which is in the interests of all the producers but above all in the national interest.

'So the State will be making use of individual expertise and self-interest in the higher interests of the nation.'

Source: A. Lyttelton (ed), *Italian Fascisms from Pareto to Gentile* (London: Jonathan Cape, 1973), p. 295.

---

improving land which was to be cultivated by new peasant farmers.

None of these measures actually worked, and probably could not work. Some, but not many and certainly not enough, new farming communities were set up on reclaimed land; large landowners, especially in the south, refused to co-operate in the schemes, and the government did not want to force them and so make enemies of them. The declining birth rate and the movement of people from the countryside to urban industrial areas continued, and from the experience of most industrial and industrialising countries the two things seemed to go together. Mussolini praised the southern Italian region of Basilicata as being the most 'advanced' in Italy because it had the highest birth rate, when in fact it was one of the country's poorest and most economically backward areas. 'Ruralisation' remained the official policy of Fascism at the very point in the mid-1930s when Italy became an industrial country, in the sense of more people being employed in industry than in agriculture.

The Corporate State

The 1926 syndical law was meant to be a step on the way to creating an economy organised on corporate lines. A new Ministry of Corporations was set up in 1926, long before corporations actually existed, but progress was rather slow, which was a sign of the objections to corporatism made by employers' organisations like *Confindustria*. A kind of consultative corporative assembly, the National Council of Corporations, was established in 1930, and in 1934 22 corporations, one for each branch of trade, industry and agriculture, finally appeared. The timing was not a coincidence. The world was hardly recovering from the Great Depression, which made people question whether a capitalist economic system could and should survive. Fascism propagandised the corporate state inside and outside Italy as the answer to the crisis of capitalism which avoided the extremes of Communism in Russia. It was the nearest Italian Fascism got to claiming that it was a political system which was not just Italian, but universal, a system which had found the answer to managing

A poster representing the 'freedom' and 'dignity' of manual labour in the new Italy, 'free' to increase national production once the 'chains' of socialism and strikes have been broken. Fascism always emphasised the production rather than the distribution of national wealth

the social and economic problems of modern life and could be adopted in other countries as well.

In the event, Italy's employers did not have to worry too much about the corporations. As the meeting places of everybody involved in the process of production, they were meant to co-ordinate and organise the various sectors of the economy. In reality, employers tended to come out on top, because their representatives in the corporations were actual employers or managers, with a concrete expertise and interest to defend, while the workers' representatives were not elected or nominated by the workers themselves but were appointed by the State and were PNF, syndicate or government officials. The representatives of the Ministry of Corporations, standing for the consumers and the 'national interest', were state officials as well. The corporations' composition showed that there was a lack of balance in the Fascist system, in that the interests of employers were usually bound to prevail over the interests of workers.

State Control of the Economy

It was not just a matter of the way the corporations were run. The corporations never became the bodies which actually took decisions on production; they never, in other words, ran the economy. The Fascist state certainly intervened more in economic affairs during and as a result of the Great Depression, and this intervention came close to state control if not planning of the economy in the late 1930s when autarchy became official policy. But the corporations were not really the organisations through which the State directed the economy. So when, in 1931-2, at the height of the Depression, the government decided it had to save now bankrupt industries and the big banks which had lent money to them, the organisation eventually set up to do this in 1933 was the Institute of Industrial Reconstruction (IRI). This was, in effect, a huge state firm. It paid off with taxpayers' money the debts of the private banks and industries and took over the shares, and therefore the ownership of the failing industries. Some of them were eventually returned to the private sector, but IRI became a permanent body, not just a temporary way of saving industries during the Depression, and held on to iron and steel, shipbuilding and navigation companies, among others. Overall, IRI came to control firms whose combined value was about one-fifth of the total for the country, which meant that only the Soviet Union in Europe had a bigger share of the economy under state control than Fascist Italy. The same thing happened in other parts of the economy. Public bodies or agencies, today we call them quangos, were set up to organise and run sectors of the economy, usually staffed by managers and businessmen from companies in the sector concerned, initially because of the Depression and then to put into effect the autarchic aims of the government in the late 1930s.

A Compromising Dictatorship

By 1929 the erection of a repressive dictatorship was basically finished. Fascism claimed to be 'totalitarian', but there were doubts that it was really so at this point, and most historians doubt that Fascism was ever capable of being 'totalitarian'. This was because of the compromises Fascism had made with important interests and institutions, in order both to come to power and to stay in power. So the industrial employers' organisation, *Confindustria*, had to join and work in corporate bodies, which it disliked, but was reassured by the fact that employers could dominate them and their powers to run the economy were limited. At this time, anyway, there was no sense of Fascism's new organs being a threat to the management of their businesses, which was what really concerned them. The King's powers were weakened by constitutional changes like the law creating the position of Head of Government, and he was continually in the shade of Mussolini throughout the 1930s. But Mussolini had not yet abolished the monarchy, and the King remained the official head of state who could dismiss and appoint the Head of Government and was still, just, the commander-in-chief of the armed forces. But Mussolini calculated that keeping the King as head of state, at least for the time being, helped him to secure the loyalty of the army and the state bureaucracy.

The Lateran Pacts

Similar concerns were behind Mussolini's agreement with the Catholic Church in the Lateran Pacts, which were signed in February 1929 after nearly three years of secret and difficult negotiations, and included a Concordat dealing with Church-State relations. This agreement officially ended the

The Pope and Mussolini sign the Concordat, 1929

The Lateran Pacts ●

In the famous painting by Diego Rivera, which refers to the 1929 agreement between the Vatican and the Fascist government, Pope Pius XI shows his support for Mussolini with an ambiguous gesture which is half way between a blessing and a crossing of the fingers. The figure in the bottom right, about to be stabbed, is Matteotti

● **The Lateran Pacts**

hostility between the Church and the Italian state which had existed since the country's unification, and brought Mussolini enormous prestige both in Italy and outside. Catholics were now encouraged by the Church to support the Fascist government. But Catholic support had a price; the Concordat recognised the right to exist and organise of Catholic Action, the name given to a vast nationwide network of Catholic bodies involving people of all ages in a wide range of social activities. Through Catholic Action, the Church had a place in the social life of millions of Italians. As a result of the Concordat, Catholic Action was the only non-Fascist organisation legally allowed to exist in Fascist Italy, and as such it was a very big 'hole' in the 'totalitarian' state. Mussolini recognised this, but as with the monarchy, he thought that the Catholic Church was too established and important an institution to be tackled head-on, in a confrontational way. What he was attempting to do was to connect or associate these powerful independent institutions with the Fascist state, get them on his side. At least in the short term, the tactic worked. There was always competition and rivalry between Catholic and Fascist youth organisations in the 1930s over the control of young people, which erupted in 1931 with Fascists attacking Catholic members and premises and the government temporarily closing down Catholic clubs. But the dispute was patched up, and the Concordat remained in place. The Church disliked and criticised the race laws of 1938, but generally supported most of the government's policies, from 'ruralisation' and the births campaign to corporatism and the conquest of empire.

Mussolini's Personal Rule

But we cannot really leave things there, if we want to catch what was special about the Fascist dictatorship as it went into the 1930s. For one thing, Mussolini developed a personal style of rule, which in some ways was not like the way Hitler did things in Nazi Germany. Mussolini certainly concentrated power, or rather responsibility, in his own hands. In 1929 Mussolini was Head of Government and also headed eight out of 13 government ministries. He gave some of these up between 1929 and 1932, but by 1933 he was again at the head of seven ministries. This was an extraordinary workload for one man, and he certainly did not and could not do all the work, although he certainly wanted to give the impression that there was no aspect of government and policy that was not under his control and that he worked day and night on the nation's affairs. In practice, much of the work in the ministries was done by the junior ministers, though having Mussolini as their direct ministerial boss probably prevented them from showing much initiative. This might be one reason why sometimes things did not get done. Hitler, by contrast, was lazy, hated the bureaucratic chores of office and did as little paperwork as possible, and did not accumulate government and party positions, allowing other top Nazis like Goebbels, Goering, Himmler, Ley and Ribbentrop to build up administrative and political empires of their own.

Mussolini disliked and mistrusted other people, and thought that most of them were corrupt or corruptible, and this contributed to the often incompetent and superficial way in which the Fascist state was run. By 1932 most Fascists of ability and political importance were no longer in major government or PNF posts and some were in personal and political disgrace. The appointment of people with less ability happened so often as to suggest that it was a deliberate policy to keep out of office Fascists who might take some of the attention away from Mussolini. The obvious incompetence of many top men in the 1930s seemed to confirm Mussolini's cynical view of human nature, made him even less willing to open himself to the criticism or advice of his government colleagues, and made him feel even more isolated and indispensable in his position as Head of Government. Significantly, Mussolini never allowed the Grand Council to operate as the decision-making forum of the Fascist state. It became a rubber stamp, simply meeting to approve decisions which had already been taken, and some major policy decisions were made by Mussolini without it meeting at all. Nobody mentioned the Council's right to nominate a successor to Mussolini; Mussolini *was* Fascism. In this way the personal will of the dictator undermined the Fascist body which had been set up to make sure that Fascism would last.

Mussolini's sense of isolation, of being alone in charge of the nation's affairs, was strengthened by the deliberate creation of the 'myth', the glorified ideal, of Mussolini as *Duce*, or Leader. 'Mussolini is always right' was the slogan adopted by the PNF in the late 1920s, and from this point the propaganda image of Mussolini was of the selfless, all-powerful and all-knowing leader, single-handedly creating the new Italy. This rather detached and inhuman image of the *Duce*, a Leader of more than normal talents and drive, above and beyond the normal little concerns of life did, in a way, actually fit the self-imposed solitude or loneliness of Mussolini in government.

The PNF

However, to put too great an emphasis on Mussolini's personal dictatorship can be misleading. Fascism, as a system of rule, was more than the will of the dictator. When the PNF became in 1925-6 the only party which was allowed to exist in the Fascist state, new membership was open only to young men who came through the Fascist youth organisations. For Fascists like Farinacci, the PNF was an elite organisation and should remain so, its members limited to those who had joined the movement in the early days and the young men trained up in the youth bodies. But in 1932, to mark the tenth anniversary celebrations of Fascism in power, the Fascist party was thrown open to anybody who wanted to apply, or who had to apply: PNF membership was made a requirement for getting a job in central and local government and for getting promotion as a government employee. The party, rather than be an elite, was to become the nation. PNF membership rose from about one million in 1932 to nearly two million in 1934 and over two and a half million

Document 8c. Carlo Scorza, the head of the PNF's youth organisations, reports to Mussolini in 1931 about the kind of young men being formed in those organisations.

'The Duce and the Regime do not need thinking brains which get lost in abstractions … The Duce needs to have ready to respond to any order, an army organised in closed ranks: huge and imposing, firm and disciplined, masculine, unshakeable in faith, irresistible in its advance; in short, an armed religious order.'

Source: A. Aquarone, *L'Organizzazione dello stato totalitario* (Turin: Einaudi, 1965), pp. 514-5.

in 1939, about six per cent of the total population.

The PNF did not only become a 'mass' party in terms of membership. It also took on the job of organising the whole nation. Especially under the leadership of Achille Starace, a long-standing Fascist of limited ability but personally loyal to Mussolini and with an almost manic commitment to order and regimentation, the PNF developed and extended a national network of organisations which reached down into local areas and involved large numbers of people in a wide range of activities it sponsored and controlled, from welfare to recreation and sport. The PNF wanted to set up an efficient organisational system through which people could be controlled and, more importantly, through which their support for the Fascist government could be gained. The aim was through organisation and propaganda within the organisations to get people to identify with Fascism and its goals, and to get them to do so in an active and enthusiastic way. In other words, the aim was to 'Fascistise' Italians, make them Fascist. It was in this sense that Fascism claimed to be 'totalitarian', and that the PNF carried out its functions in the service of the Fascist state. So, in the 1930s, the PNF attempted to organise in areas and among social groups which, up to then, had been hostile to Fascism, or simply were not interested in or aware of Fascism. It tried to cover the south and the islands, and the remoter rural areas of the country; it recruited among industrial and agricultural workers, young people, women of different social classes and backgrounds, all of them as yet largely untouched by Fascism or with no reason to be attracted to it. For some women living in the south, this was the first time that anybody had tried to organise them.

The Young

Of course, it is very difficult to measure how effective these organisations were in building up support for Fascism. The State and PNF Fascist youth organisations, combined under the PNF's control in 1937, probably made the biggest impression on their members, since young people, simply because they were young, were not yet 'formed' in their behaviour and attitudes and had not known or experienced any other kind of political system than Fascism. The youth organisations provided physical exercise and training of

Ducument 8d. The leader of the Italian Communist party, Palmiro Togliatti, giving a talk in exile in Moscow in the mid-1930s, recognises the appeal of the *Dopolavoro* to workers.

'What do the local Dopolavoros do? They carry on a whole series of activities. The benefits the workers have are manifold. They get special terms, reductions for theatre and film tickets, discounts on food and clothing bought in certain department stores, on outings. Then they also have some form of welfare.'

Source: J. Whittam, *Fascist Italy* (Manchester: Manchester University Press, 1995), p. 159.

a military kind, with lots of drilling, parading and 'playing soldiers', and organised sports events and trips, including summer camp holidays at the seaside or the mountains. The Fascist government certainly thought that the Fascist youth movement was the most important of all the PNF organisations, because if it could control and form the new generation then Fascism would survive in the future. Mussolini expected that the influence and hold on Italian society of non-Fascist institutions like the Catholic Church would eventually be worn away once the nation's youth were regimented and their attitudes shaped in these organisations. The way to beat the Church, in other words, was by out-organising their Catholic Action rivals.

Workers

One of the biggest and most popular 'mass' organisations was the *Dopolavoro*, or National Afterwork Organisation, which had over three and a half million members by 1939 and a wide social appeal, its members including peasants, industrial workers and white collar employees. The *Dopolavoro* organised or made arrangements for filling the leisure time of working adults, and did a lot to introduce people to what are now normal leisure time activities, going to see films, listening to the radio, playing and watching sport, going on trips and holidays, even going shopping. There was not much obvious Fascist propaganda and indoctrination going on here. But the *Dopolavoro*, like no other Fascist organisation, involved people such as industrial workers who had a good reason to dislike and resent Fascism for its demolition of labour unions. Enjoying some of the facilities and opportunities for recreation offered by the *Dopolavoro* at least made them see Fascism in a more favourable light.

The Attempts to 'Fascistise' Italy

In the 1930s Mussolini's foreign policy decisions, dealt with in the next chapter, affected Fascism's internal policies. This was particularly the case from 1936, when Italy's invasion and conquest of the East African country, Ethiopia, in 1935-6 led to the the two Fascist powers in Europe, Fascist Italy and Nazi Germany, coming closer together. What was called the 'Axis' in 1936 became a military and political alliance between Italy and Germany in May 1939, called 'the Pact of Steel'. Running alongside the Axis between 1936

Document 8e. The 'Fascistisation' of Italians begins to affect the way they speak, in this comment by the PNF in 1938 on the decision to ban the use of the polite form of 'you'.

'Now the Revolution must have an impact on "habits" ... The abolition of the use of the servile and foreign "*lei*", detested by all the great Italians, is of the greatest importance. Other steps will have to be taken in this area, and it will be easy to overcome the residual scepticism of those idiots in our own country and abroad who would prefer the easygoing, disorganised, amusing, mandolin-strumming Italy of the past rather than the organised, solid, silent and powerful Italy of the Fascist era.'

Source: G. Bonfanti, *Il Fascismo 2 Il regime* (Brescia: La Scuola, 1977), p. 152.

and 1939, the Fascist government increased the efforts to 'Fascistise' Italian society, which reached a peak in the so-called 'anti-bourgeois' campaign of 1938-9. This campaign was not really aimed at the middle classes as a socio-economic group. Most of Fascism's early and continuing support came from middle-class people. The point of the campaign was to attack what were seen as typical middle-class or 'bourgeois' habits and attitudes which could appear in any and all social groups. The middle-class mentality was that of the couch potato, lazy, peaceloving, materialistic, all for comfort and the quiet life and taking things for granted, the exact opposite of the proper Fascist out-look. So the Fascist party started some laughable campaigns to change people's conduct and attitudes in a more aggressive and warlike direction. As Mussolini said in 1938, 'from now on, the revolution must have an effect on the habits of Italians. They must learn to be less sympathetic in order to become hard, relentless and hateful - in other words, masters'. Civil servants had to wear a uniform at work, while the Militia and the army adopted the goose-step to march by. The handshake was banned as unhygienic; people had to greet each other with the stiff raised arm of the Fascist salute. People were not meant to use the polite form for saying 'you', *lei* in Italian, because it was a foreign influence on the Italian language and showed that the person using it was meek and servile; the proper way to address someone else was *voi*, much more virile, comradely and 'Italian'.

Anti-Jewish Measures

People probably could not take much of this seriously. The anti-Jewish Fascist race laws introduced in 1938 were another matter. These measures discriminated against Jews in Italy, banning sex and marriage between 'Aryan' Italians and Jews, who did not belong to the Italian race, and banning Jews from the PNF and all jobs in the public sector, including education, the army and the bureaucracy. Jews were not allowed to join or work in the pro-fessions, and be lawyers, doctors and so on, and could not own or inherit property. Historians can still not agree on why anti-Semitic action was taken, especially when the number of Jews in Italy were small and they were well-

Document 8f. Mussolini justifies the regime's race policy in a speech of September 1938.

'The racial problem … is related to our conquest of the Empire; for history teaches that empires are won by arms, but held by prestige. And prestige demands a clear-cut racial consciousness which is based not only on difference but on the most definite superiority.'

Source: C.F. Delzell (ed), *Mediterranean Fascism, 1919-1945. Selected Documents* (London: Macmillan, 1971), p. 177.

integrated into normal Italian life. Many historians assume that it was something to do with Nazi Germany. But there was no sign of the German Nazis trying to get the Italians to take on the race issue and so remove what everybody saw as the biggest difference between Fascism and Nazism. The Germans were as surprised as everyone else at the measures, though they welcomed them and thought, as did most people in Italy, that they made the relationship between Italy and Germany stronger. So one view is that Mussolini made Fascism racist in order to show that he was serious about the Axis with Germany and wanted relations to be even closer. But there was probably another reason behind the measures. Italy had just conquered Ethiopia, enlarging its empire in East Africa. To Mussolini, Italians had to be capable in mind and body to rule an empire and peoples of a different race; they needed to become 'imperialist' in outlook, have a sense of their own racial superiority, of their right to dominate others, and this applied in their own country as well as in African colonies. Racism was, from this point of view, part of the more general campaign of the time to speed up the 'Fascistisation' of the Italian people; learning to hate Jews was part of the toughening up process to make Italians 'hard', fit for war and empire.

Autarchy and Preparation for War

The connection between foreign policy and domestic policy in the 'Fascistisation' campaign of the late 1930s, can also be seen in the government's economic policy of autarchy, marked by the State's increasing intervention in the economy. State and large private companies co-operated in spending public money on military equipment and materials, and developing Italian resources of fuel and raw materials and synthetic home-produced products like artificial fibres, in order to replace goods imported from other countries. The government agency which had been set up for the invasion of Ethiopia to handle foreign trade by controlling the kind and amounts of imports and the foreign currency needed to pay for imports, became a full government ministry in 1937. Many Italian businesses relied on imported raw materials to manufacture their products, and found that it was now the government and not them which decided what would be imported and how much. From 1936-7 the government tried to control the production and supply of basic agricultural foodstuffs and raw materials by obliging farmers to

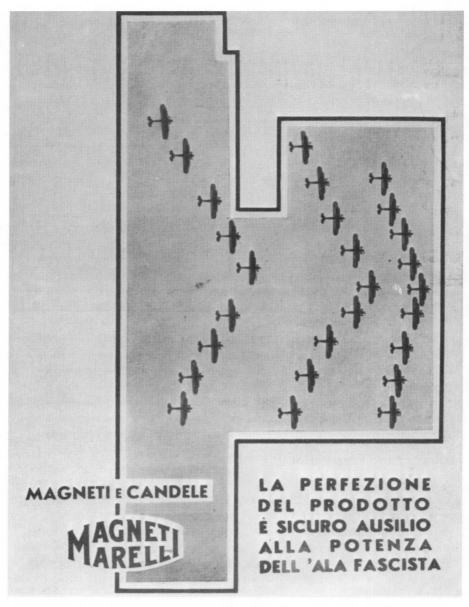

MAGNETI E CANDELE

MAGNETI MARELLI

LA PERFEZIONE
DEL PRODOTTO
È SICURO AUSILIO
ALLA POTENZA
DELL 'ALA FASCISTA

An advertisement which says: 'Magnetos and Sparking Plugs, Magneti Marelli. The perfect quality of the product is guaranteed to strengthen the power of the Fascist Air Force.' The advertisement is interesting for its design (the planes are flying within an outline of the lictor's rod), the open use of a political symbol to promote a business, and thus for the connection it makes between Fascism and business. Magneti Marelli, a Milan-based engineering company, supplied electrical parts for Fiat and radio manufacturers. It was the sole supplier of its type of product to the Italian Air Force and benefited from rearmament and autarchy policies

Document 8f. Mussolini justifies the regime's race policy in a speech of September 1938.

'The racial problem … is related to our conquest of the Empire; for history teaches that empires are won by arms, but held by prestige. And prestige demands a clear-cut racial consciousness which is based not only on difference but on the most definite superiority.'

Source: C.F. Delzell (ed), *Mediterranean Fascism, 1919-1945. Selected Documents* (London: Macmillan, 1971), p. 177.

---

integrated into normal Italian life. Many historians assume that it was something to do with Nazi Germany. But there was no sign of the German Nazis trying to get the Italians to take on the race issue and so remove what everybody saw as the biggest difference between Fascism and Nazism. The Germans were as surprised as everyone else at the measures, though they welcomed them and thought, as did most people in Italy, that they made the relationship between Italy and Germany stronger. So one view is that Mussolini made Fascism racist in order to show that he was serious about the Axis with Germany and wanted relations to be even closer. But there was probably another reason behind the measures. Italy had just conquered Ethiopia, enlarging its empire in East Africa. To Mussolini, Italians had to be capable in mind and body to rule an empire and peoples of a different race; they needed to become 'imperialist' in outlook, have a sense of their own racial superiority, of their right to dominate others, and this applied in their own country as well as in African colonies. Racism was, from this point of view, part of the more general campaign of the time to speed up the 'Fascistisation' of the Italian people; learning to hate Jews was part of the toughening up process to make Italians 'hard', fit for war and empire.

Autarchy and Preparation for War

The connection between foreign policy and domestic policy in the 'Fascistisation' campaign of the late 1930s, can also be seen in the government's economic policy of autarchy, marked by the State's increasing intervention in the economy. State and large private companies co-operated in spending public money on military equipment and materials, and developing Italian resources of fuel and raw materials and synthetic home-produced products like artificial fibres, in order to replace goods imported from other countries. The government agency which had been set up for the invasion of Ethiopia to handle foreign trade by controlling the kind and amounts of imports and the foreign currency needed to pay for imports, became a full government ministry in 1937. Many Italian businesses relied on imported raw materials to manufacture their products, and found that it was now the government and not them which decided what would be imported and how much. From 1936-7 the government tried to control the production and supply of basic agricultural foodstuffs and raw materials by obliging farmers to

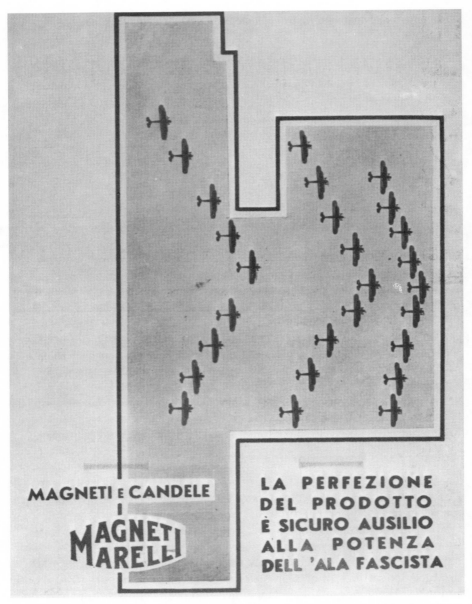

An advertisement which says: 'Magnetos and Sparking Plugs, Magneti Marelli. The perfect quality of the product is guaranteed to strengthen the power of the Fascist Air Force.' The advertisement is interesting for its design (the planes are flying within an outline of the lictor's rod), the open use of a political symbol to promote a business, and thus for the connection it makes between Fascism and business. Magneti Marelli, a Milan-based engineering company, supplied electrical parts for Fiat and radio manufacturers. It was the sole supplier of its type of product to the Italian Air Force and benefited from rearmament and autarchy policies

hand over their produce to government depots at prices fixed by the government. This kind of requisitioning, along with the other measures of state economic control, and the increased pace of 'Fascistisation', however effective or not they might have been, showed that the government was attempting to equip the country for war.

Overall, the effect of more aggressive Fascist foreign and internal policies in the late 1930s was to damage the compromises with those bodies and institutions which Mussolini's dictatorship had made in the late 1920s. Some of the businesses belonging to *Confindustria* made a huge amount of money from government spending on autarchy and on the military. But there was a price to pay in greater state control of the economy, which in some ways prevented businessmen from making their own management decisions about production. The Catholic Church criticised the race laws, and generally resented the way that despite the Concordat the Fascist party increased its efforts to organise the population in rivalry with Catholic Action. The point in the late 1930s when Fascism was becoming most Fascist in its foreign and domestic policies was also the time when important Italian institutions began to feel really anxious about where Mussolini was taking the country. Once Italy did badly in the war, which it joined in 1940, they started to move away from supporting Fascism and welcomed the King's overthrow of Mussolini in 1943.

Questions to Consider

- With which groups in Italian society did Mussolini have to compromise in order to increase his power?
- Was Italy a totalitarian state?
- Was the 'Corporate State' a success?
- Which of Mussolini's policies do you consider were successes and which were failures?
- How far was Mussolini's rule a *personal* rule?
- Was the PNF a *political* party in the 1930s?
- Why, in your view, did Mussolini introduce anti-Semitism in 1938?

9 Foreign Policy, 1922-40

A look at the foreign policy of Fascist Italy is the best way to close the main part of this account of Italy between the two world wars. This is because the foreign policy decisions taken by Mussolini in the 1930s revealed most about the nature and aims of Fascism and did most to determine the fall of the Fascist regime. This chapter should really be read alongside the previous chapter on the Fascist state, since the measures taken within Italy for the greater 'Fascistisation' of the country only make sense if they are connected to the increasingly aggressive and dangerous line of Mussolini's foreign policy. It is, of course, unwise to treat the foreign policy of any modern state as if it was entirely separate from domestic pressures and policies. But the connections and inter-dependence between internal and foreign policies were especially strong in the case of the two Fascist states of Italy and Germany in the 1930s. The 'totalitarian' state and an imperialistic foreign policy went hand in hand, the one strengthening the other in a kind of cycle. The 'totalitarian' system controlled and disciplined the country in preparation for wars of conquest and expansion, creating the internal order and unity without which no people could successfully go to war. A successful war in turn justified and validated the continued controls of the State, and reinforced the order, morale and will of the people, the basis of the next expansionist move. The internal order of the 'totalitarian' state was both and, at the same time, the reason for and the result of war.

Continuity in Foreign Policy?

This interpretation of what made the foreign policies of the Fascist states so dynamic and aggressive is not one which is accepted by all historians, and the disagreement among them over the aims and methods of Mussolini's foreign policy is another good reason for making this the closing chapter. The famous British historian, A.J.P. Taylor, shocked many people at the time when in his book on *The Origins of the Second World War*, he described the Nazi dictator, Hitler, as a 'normal' German statesman. He meant by this that Hitler had aims to make Germany great, which were really no different from the foreign policy aims of the men who had governed and led the country before him, both under the German monarchy or empire of 1871-1918 and the parliamentary Weimar republic of 1918-33. Taylor was arguing that there was a basic *continuity* in German foreign policy from the late nineteenth century into the twentieth century. The debate about Mussolini's foreign policy is around the same theme of continuity, the extent to which he kept to or moved away from the policy of the liberal governments of Italy before 1922, whether it is possible, in other words, to speak of a 'Fascist' foreign policy.

Italian Foreign Policy before Fascism

In order to understand Mussolini's foreign policy, then, we need to know something about the foreign policy of liberal Italy after the unification of the country in 1871. Any country's foreign policy, its relations with other countries, were and are affected by its geographical and strategic position, and by its economic resources, which determine whether it is relatively strong or weak as a military force. Italy's capacity to defend itself against other countries, let alone expand and gain territory, was always limited by being a peninsular with long and vulnerable coastlines and not being as strong economically as the other industrialised and industrialising nations in the late nineteenth century. This was why Italy has been described as 'least of the Great Powers' or 'the greatest of the small powers', and why one of the most consistent aims of her foreign policy was to have friendly relations with Britain, the country with the largest navy and from whom she imported the bulk of her coal supplies.

If Italy had an 'enemy', then it was France. There were territorial disputes and fears which lingered on from Italy's unification: France had been given Savoy and Nice by Piedmont as the price for France fighting against the Austrians in northern Italy in 1858-9, and Italy was for a while afraid that the Pope would seek French help to recover the state he had lost to Italy in 1870. There were also damaging trade wars with France in the 1880s, which badly hit Italy's agricultural exports, and on-going colonial disputes in North and East Africa which partly lay behind Italy's failed attempt to extend her East African territory to Abyssinia (Ethiopia) in the 1890s and her successful conquest of Libya from the Turkish empire in 1911-12. Colonial rivalry was really about whether Italy or France would control the Western Mediterranean. So even though Italy claimed territory in the north-east which was part of the Austrian empire, she joined the so-called Triple Alliance with Germany and Austria-Hungary in 1882, a mutually defensive alliance against France which was still in operation at the time of the outbreak of the First World War in 1914.

Italy might have wanted to be a Great Power like Britain, France and Germany, and the acquisition of African colonies was an attempt to play the part of a Great Power. But generally, Italy played safe and was unadventurous, a role in line with her strategic vulnerability and relative economic weakness. Some nationalists and liberals wanted more, and either looked to Italy completing her national unification in the north-east and gaining influence in the Adriatic and the Balkans at Austria's expense, or expanding her colonies in Africa in order to compete with France in the Mediterranean.

The First World War

The outbreak of the First World War in 1914 opened up certain opportunities as well as dangers for Italy as a middle-rank European power which could not really act independently in international relations but which could manoeuvre between the Great Powers when they came into conflict with each other. Italy was neutral in 1914, not joining the war on either side, which was allowable under the terms of the Triple Alliance. But the Prime Minister, Salandra, negotiated with both sides for the best deal, which was provided by France and Britain in the secret Treaty of London which brought Italy into the war against Germany and Austria in 1915. Italy was promised the Trentino, Trieste and South Tyrol to extend her north-eastern frontier, and the Balkan slav areas of Istria and northern Dalmatia, which would allow Italy to control the Adriatic and become a power in the Balkans. These were the hopes which were disappointed at the 1919 Versailles peace conference at the end of the war, when Italy gained her natural geographical borders but was refused the expected gains in the Adriatic. Under the Treaty of Rappallo, which Giolitti negotiated with the new Yugoslav state in late 1920, Italy got Trieste and Istria, but not all she wanted in Dalmatia.

Fascist Foreign Policy in the 1920s and Early 1930s

Fascism was imperialist from the start, and attacked both the post-war liberal governments and Italy's wartime allies for Italy's 'mutilated victory', the failure to achieve the expected gains after the war. Mussolini made no secret before and after 1922 of his desire to make Italy a Great Power through empire and control of the Mediterranean. But how was this to be done? Some historians say that Mussolini behaved, indeed had to behave, in international relations in a way which was not basically different from his predecessors in government. They argue that Italian foreign policy in the 1920s and early 1930s was as moderate and unadventurous as before, not risking friendship with Britain and no real challenge to the dominance in Europe of Britain and France. There was more bluster and noise coming from Mussolini, but this was largely a way of impressing Italians that Italy under Fascism was a force in international affairs, and did not mark any change in direction of foreign policy. The areas where Fascist Italy wanted to spread Italian power and influence in the world were essentially those of pre-Fascist liberal Italy, towards the Adriatic and the Balkans, and towards Mediterranean Africa, and the obstacle in both cases was France.

Nothing new here, then, and the same historians also argue for a continuity of method as well as of aims. Since Mussolini could not really change the factors of strategic and relative economic and military weakness which prevented Italy from making a big splash internationally, the best and only option was to do what Salandra had done in 1914-15. Italy had to move between the more powerful countries, taking advantage of their rivalries and conflicts and making herself available at a price to both sides without fully committing herself to any one side. In the words of Italy's Fascist Foreign Minister between 1929 and 1932, Dino Grandi, Italy was to be the 'determining weight' in international relations, in other words, not one of the major players but the bit player who could tip the balance for one side or the other and demand something for doing so.

The continuity argument has some validity. But it probably overestimates the 'moderation' of Mussolini's foreign policy in the first ten years of Fascist government. Fascist Italy wanted to 'revise' the post-war Versailles settlement and extend Italy's influence in Eastern Europe, where she faced France's network of alliances with Czechoslovakia, Poland, Romania and Yugoslavia, new, restored and enlarged countries which had all gained from the post-war treaties and the break-up of the Austrian empire. Mussolini caused trouble in the region by supporting the 'revisionist' claims of other states, especially Hungary, against those which had benefited from the post-war settlement. He also tried to undermine these countries in Eastern Europe, particularly Yugoslavia, which was a new state containing different ethnic and religious groups, by supporting and arming movements which wanted their national groups to break away and form their own states.

In the most dramatic action of his early years of government, Mussolini ordered the attack and occupation of the Greek island of Corfu in 1923 in a dispute with Greece, hoping to annex it to Italy and control the Adriatic coastline. This action is often seen as the exception which proved the rule of Mussolini's decent conduct in foreign relations in the 1920s, but it can also be seen as the most spectacular example of Mussolini's disturbing behaviour during this period. He had to evacuate the island when Britain appeared to be ready to send its Mediterranean fleet. This was the real hard lesson of Corfu, that Mussolini at this point could not challenge British naval strength in the Mediterranean, nor French influence in the Balkans. It was not so much that Mussolini was 'moderate' in the 1920s, as that his ambitions were effectively checked by British and French control of European affairs, an international situation which Italy was not powerful enough to change on her own.

The Invasion and Conquest of Ethiopia

What changed the situation was the coming to power in Germany of a nationalist government under Hitler in 1933, a very direct challenge to Britain and particularly France in Europe. Here was a balance between the major European countries which Italy could hope to exploit for her own advantage. Mussolini had ordered the Colonial Minister to start planning for an Italian invasion of Ethiopia, the site of Italy's disastrous colonial defeat in the 1890s, in 1932. The invasion only went ahead, however, once circumstances in Europe changed as a consequence of Hitler's coming to power in Germany. A failed Nazi coup in Austria in 1934, which was intended to lead to the union of Austria with Germany and would have brought Germany to Italy's

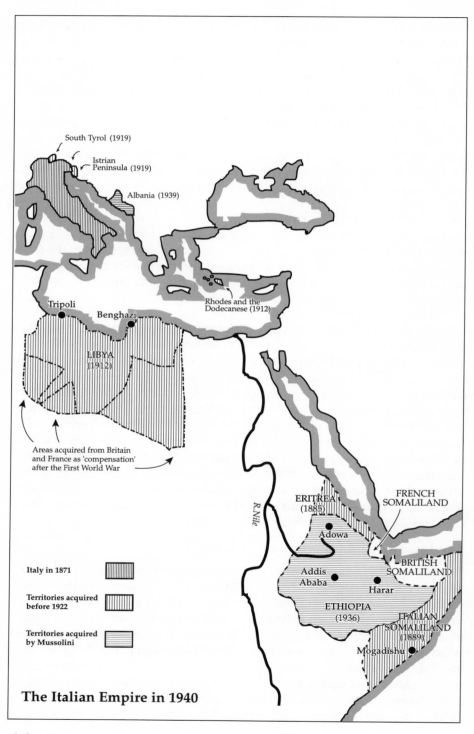

South Tyrol (1919)

Istrian
Peninsula (1919)

Albania (1939)

Tripoli

Benghazi

Rhodes and the
Dodecanese (1912)

LIBYA
(1912)

Areas acquired from Britain
and France as 'compensation'
after the First World War

R.Nile

ERITREA
(1885)

FRENCH
SOMALILAND

Adowa

BRITISH
SOMALILAND

Addis
Ababa

Harar

ETHIOPIA
(1936)

ITALIAN
SOMALILAND
(1889)

Mogadishu

Italy in 1871

Territories acquired
before 1922

Territories acquired
by Mussolini

The Italian Empire in 1940

Documents 9a. Mussolini announces the conquest of Ethiopia (Abyssinia), in a speech of May 1936. Note the attempt to evoke the empire of Ancient Rome.

'Italy has her empire at last: a Fascist empire because it bears the indestructible tokens of the will and of the power of the Roman lictors ... An empire of civilization and humanity for all the populations of Abyssinia. That is the tradition of Rome, who, after victory, associated the peoples with their destiny.'

Source: C.J. Lowe and F. Marzari, *Italian Foreign Policy, 1870-1940* (London: Routledge, 1975), p. 406.

9b. The German ambassador to Italy reports back to the German Foreign Ministry his conversation with Mussolini in January 1936, where Mussolini effectively agrees to Austria becoming a 'German' state.

'... he (Mussolini) thought it would now be possible to achieve a fundamental improvement in German-Italian relations and to dispose of the only dispute, namely, the Austrian problem ... The simplest method would be for Berlin and Vienna themselves to settle their relations ... in the form of a treaty of friendship ... which would in practice bring Austria into Germany's wake, so that she could pursue no other foreign policy than one parallel with that of Germany. If Austria, as a formally quite independent state, were thus in practice to become a German satellite, he would have no objection.'

Source: C.J. Lowe and F. Marzari, *Italian Foreign Policy, 1870-1940* (London: Routledge, 1975), p. 405.

---

northern borders, finally pushed Mussolini into an understanding with France in early 1935. France accepted that Italy would control Ethiopia and, in return, Italy would support France in Europe against Germany and in particular would defend Austria's independence of Germany. The diplomatic lead-up to Italy's invasion of Ethiopia can be seen as the policy of the 'determining weight' in action: Mussolini had carved out the opportunity for invasion by working on the divisions in Europe between France and Germany. The invasion was launched with almost excessive military force in October 1935; Italy fought a small colonial war with an army of 400,000 men. Mussolini declared the conquest of a Fascist empire in May 1936.

The question was now whether Italy could or would carry on the policy of playing off Germany against France and Britain without committing herself fully to one side or the other. It was certainly more difficult to do so after the conquest of Ethiopia. This was because the invasion pushed Italy apart from Britain and France, while bringing her closer to Nazi Germany. The League of Nations, the international body set up in 1919 to ensure peace and co-operation between countries, decided to impose a ban on trade with Italy, both to punish Italy for her unprovoked act of aggression against another member state and to force Italy into abandoning the invasion. Britain, as a major member of the League, supported and applied economic sanctions against Italy, arousing a wave of anti-foreigner and patriotic feeling in Italy. Germany, however, which had left the League in 1933, backed Italy during this period of international isolation, supplying her economy with coal and other materials; it appears that Hitler secretly armed the Ethiopians in order to keep the war going and so deepen the hostility between Italy and France and Britain. More significantly, with the attention of the Western powers diverted to the Ethiopian invasion, Hitler sent troops to reoccupy the Rhineland in March 1936, a move which broke the treaty of Versailles and also the Locarno treaty of 1925. Under this treaty, Italy and Britain were meant to guarantee France's borders with Germany, and so Hitler's remilitarisation of the Rhineland should have led to action against Germany. Mussolini, informed in advance by Hitler, stated that he would not support any possible League of Nations sanctions against Germany. He went further during and shortly after the period of the invasion and League sanctions, effectively telling Hitler that he would no longer oppose the future union of Austria and Germany, which eventually occurred in 1938. This was important, because it was Italian support of Austrian independence which helped to keep Italy and Germany apart and which allowed Mussolini to play off Germany and France and Britain.

The Axis and the German Alliance

So what happened during the invasion of Abyssinia in 1935-6 made it more unlikely that Mussolini would keep an equal distance between Germany and France and Britain. There was every sign, anyway, that Mussolini was choosing to associate Italy more and more with Germany after 1936. The two Fascist countries agreed to intervene in the Spanish civil war in 1936 in

A cartoon comment, captioned 'The salute of the Allied arms' in Il Popolo d'Italia *in December 1935 reflects the contrast between welcome to Italy by France and Britain in 1915 with hostility (sanctions) in 1935. Mussolini was, thereby, more ready to be seduced by Hitler*

Documents 9c. Mussolini outlines Italy's need for Mediterranean 'living space' and the place of the Axis in securing it, in a key speech to the Fascist Grand Council in February 1939.

'... Italy is surrounded by an inland sea which is connected to the oceans by the Suez Canal ... and by the straits of Gibraltar, dominated by the guns of Great Britain.

'Italy therefore does not have free access to the oceans; Italy therefore is actually a prisoner in the Mediterranean and the more populated and powerful she becomes the more she will suffer from her imprisonment.

'The bars of this prison are Corsica, Tunisia, Malta, Cyprus; the guards of this prison are Gibraltar and Suez. Corsica is a pistol pointed at the heart of Italy; Tunisia at Sicily, while Malta and Cyprus are a threat to all our positions in the central and western Mediterranean. Greece, Turkey, Egypt are all states ready to link up with Great Britain and complete the political and military encirclement of Italy ...

'... From this situation, you can draw the following conclusions:

1. The task of Italian policy, which cannot and does not have territorial aims in continental Europe except for Albania, is initially to break the bars of the prison.

2. Once the bars have been broken, Italian policy has only one direction: to march to the ocean.

'Which ocean? The Indian Ocean, connecting Libya to Ethiopia through the Sudan, or the Atlantic Ocean through French North Africa.

'In both cases, we come up against Anglo-French opposition. It is stupid to try to resolve this problem without covering our backs on the Continent. The policy of the Rome-Berlin Axis thus caters for this fundamentally important historical question.'

Source: R. De Felice, *Mussolini il Duce II Lo stato totalitario, 1936-1940* (Turin: Einaudi, 1981), pp. 321-2.

9d. The Pact of Steel of May 1939 commits the two ideologically linked fascist countries to go to war together.

'Closely bound together through internal relationships of ideologies and through comprehensive solidarity of interests, the German and Italian peoples have decided in the future to stand up side by side and with united strength in order to secure their living space ...

'... If it should happen ... that one of them becomes involved in warlike complications with another Power or ... Powers, the other ... will come to its aid as an ally and will support it with all its military forces on land, on sea, and in the air.'

Source: E. Wiskemann, *The Rome-Berlin Axis* (London: Collins, 1966), pp. 413-4.

support of the military rising against the republican government. Such discussions and agreements encouraged Mussolini to declare in November 1936 that there was now a Rome-Berlin 'Axis' in existence, indicating by this that a definite kind of collaboration in policy was emerging. The Axis was

● **The Axis and the German Alliance** 67

eventually transformed into a formal political and military alliance, the so-called 'Pact of Steel', in May 1939, which was aggressive and open-ended rather than defensive and limited in tone and content, saying that if one of them went to war the other one automatically had to go to war as well. A few months before the signing of the 'Pact of Steel', Mussolini made a very important speech to the Grand Council outlining Fascist Italy's aims in a directly anti-French and anti-British way: the final goal was dominance of the Mediterranean, both on its African and Asian shores. He pictured Italy as a prisoner in her own sea, the Mediterranean, the bars of the prison being Corsica, Tunisia (French) and Malta and Cyprus (British), the prison guards being Gibraltar (British) and the Suez Canal (French and British). The only way out was for Italy to smash her way through to the Atlantic and Indian oceans. It was this kind of statement of aims which made it unlikely that Mussolini wanted to reach some form of power-sharing arrangement with France and Britain in the Mediterranean, a recognition of Italy as a Mediterranean power. Mussolini wanted Italy to be the Mediterranean power, and this could only be achieved at the expense of French and British power and influence in the Mediterranean area. These were ambitions which were beyond Italy's capacity to realise alone; there was a certain logic, then, in Mussolini allying his country with the most powerful and expansionist power on the continent of Europe, Germany. So the Ethiopian war of 1935-6 was the occasion for a merging of aims and interests between Fascist Italy and

Goering, Mussolini, Hitler and Ciano at the Munich conference, September 1938

Document 9e Mussolini declares war in June 1940. Note the similar language to the 1939 Grand Council speech, and the same ideological dimension which appears in the Pact of Steel.

'After having solved the problem of our land frontiers, we are taking up arms to establish our sea frontiers. We want to break the territorial and military chains that are strangling us in our own sea. A nation of 45 million souls is not truly free unless it has free access to the ocean.

'This gigantic struggle is only one phase of the logical development of our revolution; … it is the struggle of young and fertile peoples against sterile ones who stand on the verge of decline; it is the struggle between two centuries and two ideas.'

Source: C.F. Delzell (ed), *Mediterranean Fascism, 1919-1945. Selected Documents* (London: Macmillan, 1971), p. 214.

Nazi Germany. Both wanted to revise the 1919 settlement, both wanted to expand their territory and power, and both were united together in hostility to France and Britain, the defenders of the 1919 settlement standing in the way of them achieving their goals. By the late 1930s, Mussolini was no more a 'normal' Italian statesman than Hitler was a 'normal' German statesman.

Relations between the two Fascist dictators were not easy, despite the existence of an alliance between Fascist Italy and Nazi Germany. It was an unequal relationship, matching the gap in economic and military capacity and potential, of power, between the two countries. There were long periods when the two men did not communicate at all, or left correspondence unanswered. Mussolini was alternately bored, impressed and beaten down by Hitler when they actually met, and Mussolini usually ended up agreeing with Hitler if only as a way of getting through the meeting, a situation not helped by Mussolini's imperfect grasp of German and his refusal to use an interpreter. Hitler often took decisions without consulting his ally, provoking Mussolini at one point to complain to his son-in-law, Galeazzo Ciano, who was Foreign Minister, that every time Hitler occupied a country, he sent him a telegram.

What alarmed both Mussolini and Ciano after the signing of the 'Pact of Steel' was the way Hitler forced the pace. They learnt in August 1939 that Hitler was planning to go war against Poland, when they had thought that war, if inevitable, would not occur for at least a few more years, giving Italy more time to prepare economically and militarily and recover from the heavy use of men and materials in the Ethiopian war and the Spanish civil war. Mussolini was now in real trouble, because he knew that Italy was probably not yet ready to join another war, and yet was bound by the terms of the Italian-German alliance to do so once his ally went to war. The face-saving way out was for Italy to stay in the alliance and provide Germany with diplomatic support, but not actually to fight. So when Germany invaded Poland in September 1939 and France and Britain declared war on Germany as a result,

Mussolini announced that Italy was 'non-belligerent'. It is important to realise that 'non-belligerence' was not the same as neutrality; it was not the repeat of 1914-15. 'Non-belligerence' meant that Italy was the ally of Germany who was not fighting at the moment. If Italy entered the war, then it would only be on Germany's side and, by March 1940, Mussolini was briefing the King that it was a matter of when and how, not whether, Italy would fight. The spectacularly rapid German military victories in France in May and June 1940 seemed to indicate that the war in Europe would soon be over and that unless Italy intervened now, Germany would be able to dictate things with or without Italy. In the expectation that Italy would only have to fight a short war in order to gain a voice in the future reorganisation of Europe, Mussolini declared war in June 1940 and invaded France.

Questions to Consider

- Was Italy a 'Great Power' or a 'small power trying to be big'?
- Are there close links between domestic policy and foreign policy?
- Were Mussolini's 'bluster and noise' actions to impress Italians or to impress the Great Powers?
- How great was the difference between Mussolini's foreign policy and that of the preceding liberal governments?
- Was conflict with Britain and France almost certain, given Mussolini's aim to turn the Mediterranean into *'Mare Nostrum'*?
- Why did Mussolini increasingly align Italy with Germany in the late 1930s?
- Was foreign policy Mussolini's downfall?

10 Postscript: Italy 1940-5

Instead of a short and victorious war, Italy fought a long and losing war, a humiliating and fatal experience for the Fascist regime which justified its existence by war and preparation for war. Mussolini hoped to fight what was called a 'parallel war', a war alongside his German ally but in different areas and for Italian aims, something he had always assumed was part of the Axis arrangement with Hitler. So the Germans would fight for their 'living space' in Northern, Central and Eastern Europe; the Italians for theirs in the Mediterranean basin.

The War and Mussolini's Fall from Power

The 'parallel war' was over by spring 1941. In October 1940, Italy invaded Greece from Albania, formally taken over by the Italians in April 1939. The Greek invasion was launched partly to prevent the Germans extending their influence in the Balkans, regarded as Italian 'living space'. It took place against the wishes of Hitler, who was afraid that a Balkan war would bring about British military intervention in the region and complicate his own preparations for a German invasion of the Soviet Union. The invasion failed miserably, and probably did more than any other event during the war to destroy the standing of the Fascist regime in the eyes of Italians and the

The invasion of Greece as seen from Athens. Little Greece resists the bully Mussolini while behind are the bound figures of Libya, Abyssinia, Albania and the Dodecanese

German ally. Hitler was forced to help Mussolini out, and German forces successfully invaded Yugoslavia and Greece in April 1941. It was just as bad in Africa. British forces and Abyssinian rebels had pushed the Italians out of their East African empire of Eritrea, Somalia and Ethiopia by May 1941, while a German army reversed initial Italian losses in Libya. These defeats marked the complete subordination of Italy to Germany in the alliance, confirmed by the Germans' growing exploitation of the Italian wartime economy. In return for essential supplies of coal, Italy exported men and agricultural produce to Germany to the extent that Italy's own industrial production and food consumption were damaged. Italy lacked the economic resources, especially fuel and raw materials, to fight a long war, without the draining away of what resources she had by her German ally.

Italy's poor showing in the war damaged Mussolini's position directly, since he was Head of Government, the Minister responsible for all three armed services, and commander-in-chief of the armed forces in the field. The 'home front' came under very great strain, as the British and Americans started to bomb the northern industrial cities in 1942, many ordinary Italians were impoverished by rising prices for increasingly scarce food and fuel unchecked by an inefficient system of rationing, and workers faced longer

A disabled German tank. Hitler's intervention could not prevent Italian defeat in North Africa

hours of work and harsh factory conditions. This, and renewed activity from left-wing anti-Fascist groups, provoked strikes by over 100,000 industrial workers in the north in March 1943, the first for nearly 20 years and a sure sign that the regime's hold on the population was slipping.

The war started to go against the Axis generally from the autumn of 1942.

A poster from wartime Italy. Italian and German helmets, united in death and victory on the field of battle. The slogan, one of Mussolini's sayings, is 'Peace with justice for all peoples'. 'Justice' for the Fascist powers, could be achieved only by war

● **The War and Mussolini's Fall from Power**

There were huge Russian counter-offensives, the Allies landed in North Africa, took Libya in May 1943, and invaded Italy itself, landing in Sicily in July 1943. Mussolini refused to take Italy out of the war and give up the German alliance. With a general loss of confidence in the Fascist regime and in Mussolini's leadership, the Grand Council met in July 1943 and passed a proposal for the King to take over military command from Mussolini, but not apparently to bring Fascism to an end. The Grand Council's action against Mussolini was rapidly overtaken by a plan eventually agreed between the King, the army command and the police chief: Mussolini was arrested and imprisoned immediately after the Grand Council meeting; the King appointed an army general, Pietro Badoglio, the commander who had finally conquered Ethiopia in 1936, as head of a military government whose first act was to ban all the organs of the Fascist state, including the PNF, the Militia and the Grand Council. The King's coup was the final price Mussolini paid for Fascism's coexistence with the monarchy in the previous 20 years.

The Salò Republic and Resistance

Badoglio declared that the war would continue on Germany's side, but nobody, least of all the Germans, was convinced. They poured troops into Italy, and occupied northern and central Italy when Badoglio, in September 1943, made public an armistice, an end to fighting with the Allies, and officially changed sides. The King and his government fled to the south to assume nominal authority in those parts of Italy now occupied by Allied troops who were fighting their way up the peninsular. Mussolini was sprung from prison by the Germans, who set him up as the head of a new Fascist government in German-occupied northern Italy, called the Italian Social Republic or the Salò Republic. Mussolini's final fling as leader was an inevitable disaster. His government was dependent on and controlled by the Germans, who fought on in Italy to defend their own country from defeat and to exploit the Italian economy for their own war effort. The Salò Republic tried to re-invent itself and go back to being the 'pure' republican and syndicalist Fascism of 1919-20, but could do little if anything concrete. So a Fascist movement which aimed to unite Italians and make the country strong internally and externally, was now in the last two years of the war just one of the 'Italies' in existence, competing in a country once again divided and occupied by foreign powers against the other 'Italies', the King's government in the south and the anti-Fascist Resistance movements in the north and centre. Mussolini moved to Milan in April 1945, as the Allies advanced and the partisans of the Resistance staged popular risings in the northern cities. Trying to escape to the Alps with a German army unit, Mussolini was stopped, recognised, 'tried' and shot by a partisan group on 27-28 April 1945.

11 Historiography

People in Britain have not lived through the experience of the breakdown of democratic politics, and Fascist dictatorship leading to war, defeat and foreign occupation, as people did in Italy and Germany between 1918 and 1945. Coming to terms with their countries' recent past was, and to an extent still is, a raw and painful issue for Italians and Germans since 1945. The different historical interpretations of Italian Fascism and German Nazism, as historians tried to understand how and why Fascism came to power in Italy and Germany, and erected 'totalitarian' regimes which plunged Europe into war, have always had a political edge and relevance greater than, for instance, the debates among British historians about the nature and 'morality' of the British government's policy of 'appeasing' the Fascist dictators in the late 1930s. The historiography of the Fascist period in Italy must, then, be related to the changes in contemporary Italian politics and society since 1945, something which the Australian historian, Richard Bosworth, usefully attempts to do in his two books mentioned in the bibliography.

'Parenthesis' or 'Revelation'?

Basically, historians of the Fascist period in Italy, as of the Nazi period in Germany, want to know how to place Fascism in the country's recent national history, an approach which of necessity takes them both back into pre-First World War liberal Italy and forward into post-1945 democratic and republican Italy, to examine the origins, impact and consequences of Fascism. They also try to place Italian Fascism among the other fascist or apparently fascist movements in interwar and wartime Europe, exploring their differences and similarities in an attempt to decide whether fascism was a European-wide phenomenon. This continuing debate about the nature and spread of fascism has become something of an academic industry, and the various generalisations about fascism range from seeing Italian Fascism, the 'first' fascism, as some kind of prototype or model for European fascism, to expressing doubts that fascism existed at all, other than in historians' minds. My remarks here will say more about the location of the Fascist period in recent Italian history, the usual historical issue of continuity and discontinuity, in other words.

Interpretations of Fascism appeared as soon as it became a force in Italian politics in the early 1920s, usually put forward by people on the socialist and democratic left who opposed Fascism and wanted to understand it so that they could fight it more effectively. From the start, there were those who argued that Fascism was to be seen as a kind of nasty and regrettable aberration or mistake, which one of Italy's most famous intellectuals, Benedetto Croce, called a 'parenthesis' in Italian history, meaning a 'gap' in Italy's development which had little relation to what happened in Italy before or afterwards. Others, alternatively, thought that Fascism was, in the words of an anti-Fascist writer of the 1920s, 'the autobiography of the nation', a movement and regime which revealed and was the near-inevitable outcome of the flawed social, economic and political development of Italy from the mid-nineteenth century *Risorgimento* onwards.

You can, I hope, see where these two sets of arguments about Fascism lead. The 'parenthesis' view literally puts the Fascist period into brackets, separating it off from what came before and what came after: Italy under its liberal political leadership between 1870 and 1915, and particularly under Giolitti in the early 1900s, was developing gradually into a modern industrial nation with democratic parliamentary institutions, keeping, in other words, to the 'normal' pattern of development of West European countries. This development was brutally interrupted by the coming to power of Fascism, the outcome of the impact of the First World War on Italian and European society, which included the Bolshevik Revolution in Russia in 1917 and the prospect that raised of socialist revolutions throughout Europe. Normal service was resumed with the military defeat of Fascism by 1945, when the country was once again able to move along the road of parliamentary democracy.

The 'revelation' line of argument certainly does not underestimate the importance of the First world War for the rise of Fascism, but lengthens the perspective on the events of the immediate post-war years in Italy: the crisis of the liberal system of government in Italy was not just down to the effects of the war; it went farther back to the imperfect process of national unification and the 'abnormal' liberal politics of the pre-war period, during which time Italians had not been made to feel members of their own nation and a huge gap had opened up between the people and their supposedly liberal state and political system. You should by now be aware that this is, basically, my reading of liberal Italy! The Marxist version of the 'revelation' view emphasises that the distribution of power between the social classes remained basically the same from liberal to Fascist Italy: the political forms certainly changed from the liberal to the Fascist state, but the dominant social and economic interests behind both were the rich and already powerful; reactionary agricultural and industrial employers had set up and financed the Fascist movement to destroy working-class organisations and to reverse the political and socio-economic gains of the organised working class in a post-war crisis of such severity that it became clear that the old liberal politicians were not up to the job. The real and lasting basis of the Fascist state was the permanent repression of the rights and interests of Italian workers.

Each of these viewpoints throws, in turn, a different light on the post-1945 situation in Italy. If Fascism was a 'parenthesis', a horrible historical accident, then it is definitely 'over' and most unlikely to occur again. However, if Fascism was the 'revelation' of Italy's recent past, then it could also be a 'revelation' of Italy's present and future, and the post-1945 Italian Republic, dominated until recently by the Catholic Christian Democrat party, could carry the same 'defects' as liberal Italy. If conditions were as 'right' as they were in the early 1920s, then the threat of Fascism might re-emerge and must be guarded against.

De Felice's Biography of Mussolini

Simplifying and generalising a lot, most interpretations of Italian Fascism tend towards one or other of these two positions, and by the 1970s the 'revelation' view was more widely held by historians. From the 1970s, however, the 'parenthesisers' have staged something of a comeback, largely as a result of the controversy in Italy aroused by the work of an Italian historian who died recently, Renzo De Felice. I am never quite sure how long it takes, and in what form, for historiographical debates to find their way into the teaching and learning of GCSE and A-Level history programmes. But I suspect that there are very few, if any, traces of the De Felice controversy in the treatment of Mussolini and Italian Fascism, compared to, for example, the contributions of Fritz Fischer and A.J.P. Taylor to debates on German foreign policy. This is nobody's fault. Starting in the mid-1960s, by 1990 De Felice had published the seventh volume of his mammoth, but still incomplete, 'life-and-times' biography of Mussolini, which in total was about 6,000 pages of dense text, the equivalent of a page to every three days of Mussolini's life. This multi-volume biography has all the appeal of an encyclopedia and, thankfully for English readers, has so far not been translated from the original Italian.

Anyway, De Felice felt it was time to challenge what he saw as the established anti-Fascist academic culture of his own country and its reading of the Fascist past, which condemned Fascism as a repressive, unpopular and war-like dictatorship, and corresponded to the post-war Italian Republic's declared foundation on anti-Fascist principles and on the 'popular' anti-Fascist Resistance of 1943-5. He thought that this official anti-Fascism made for bad history, since it led people to make political and ideological comparisons between Italy's present and recent past. He has always denied that his Mussolini biography was pro-Fascist, though his critics in Italy accuse him of this and his 'anti-anti-Fascist' history has been welcomed in Italian right-wing and neo-Fascist circles. He claimed to be writing non-political, neutral, value-free, 'objective' and 'scientific' history, and had obviously not read or taken in E.H. Carr's *What is History?* which deals with the relationship of historians to their subject matter and the way historians write themselves into their historical works. Behind this apparently non-judgmental line lay the 'parenthesis' approach: Italian Fascism was unique, distinctive, specific, and it was finished with, a phenomenon which existed and could only exist in the 1919-45 period, and therefore to be studied as 'history', not to serve some anti-Fascist political and ideological purpose. The sheer overwhelming length and detail of the biography are, in themselves, a demonstration of his belief that you first have to write Fascism's history, and only then can you interpret it. De Felice's work still causes controversy today, and his 'post-Fascist' standpoint in a sense matches the 'post-Fascist' stance of the present neo-Fascist movement, an important and now apparently legitimate and credible political force in the early 1990s, a sign for some that Italy has finally moved on from the Fascist/anti-Fascist divisions of the recent past.

The De Felice Controversy

De Felice's approach has caused argument among historians. Since he did not write off Fascism as 'bad' or 'evil', and thought that it was an 'historical fact' to be analysed 'on its own terms' and without making any prior judgement, he started taking seriously Fascist sources and what Fascists at the time said they were doing. De Felice's critics saw this as a dangerously over-literal and naive reading of 'biased' sources, which came close to passing off Fascist pro-paganda as the reality; such a failure to distinguish Fascist words from their deeds showed a lack of historical judgement and an inability to see behind the words for the 'real' meaning of Fascism. The Mussolini of De Felice's biography emerges not only as a good short-term political operator but also as a leader with a mission and a vision of making Italy great; compare this to the picture of the shallow opportunist and political manipulator whose whole regime was nothing more than a propaganda façade and who eventually came to believe his own propaganda, which emerges from Denis Mack-Smith's biography of the *Duce*.

It is often difficult to work out the De Felician line from the thousands of pages of the biography. But besides his allegedly 'objective' approach, other more specific issues have led to argument. De Felice claims that the Fascist regime enjoyed a broad base of 'consent' among the Italian people, and the period of greatest popular 'consent' was between 1929 and 1936, which were the years of the Depression as well as of the conquest of an East African empire. It is questionable whether any government was popular at a time of widespread unemployment and social distress, and De Felice does not really ask himself what kind of 'consent' or 'dissent' could exist in a dictatorship. But his views have at least obliged historians to deepen their knowledge and understanding of the Fascist regime and how it operated in the 1930s, espe-cially the 'totalitarian' organisations which were meant to mobilise people behind it.

De Felice also thinks that Italian Fascism was quite unlike German Nazism and the other fascist or apparently fascist movements of interwar Europe. Such a view allows De Felice to distance Fascism from any connection with Nazi racism and the Holocaust, and to say that Mussolini's alliance with Hitler was not driven by political and ideological similarities and aims, but was a tactical and opportunistic agreement which served Italian national interests and in practice was a strained and difficult relationship. This, in turn, is used by De Felice to argue that Mussolini's foreign policy was as moderate and realistic as his liberal predecessors, and developed without any reference to his internal policies. Mussolini saw the German Axis and alliance as a lever to gain concessions from Britain and France and a lasting accommodation of interests in the Mediterranean. In De Felice's view, Mussolini was still not committed to either side as late as the spring of 1940. Britain's short-sighted refusal to make things up with Italy and strike a deal in the Mediterranean after relations had been damaged by the Ethiopian invasion and League of Nations sanctions against Italy in 1935-6, was the reason for Mussolini being forced to lean ever closer towards Nazi Germany. In the end, De Felice is more than implying that the outbreak of war was Britain's responsibility, and that it was a war to protect Britain's empire rather than a war of the Fascist powers to create or expand their 'living space'. This is controversial stuff, and not something I agree with, as should be clear from the chapter on foreign policy. As might be expected in a biography of such complex detail and length, De Felice is not able to be consistent. How can De Felice say that Mussolini wanted agreement with Britain and France in the Mediterranean, when his most important statements of intent indicated that his aim was sole control of the 'Italian sea'? Why cannot we take at face value Mussolini's speech in this expansionist vein to the Fascist Grand Council in early 1939, which De Felice quotes at length, when he expects us to take seriously what Fascist leaders said about their activities 'on their own terms'? De Felice leaves us with a contradictory and implausible scenario; it is against both logic and reality for him to portray Mussolini acting like a conventional and pragmatic Italian statesman on the international stage while, at the same time, in Italy itself being anything but conventional and pragmatic, embarking on the attempt to remake Italy and Italians through the 'totalitarian' state. The view of 1940 as the start of an ideological, Fascist and 'totalitarian' war is much more in line with the logic and reality of Mussolini's actions at home and abroad in the 1930s.

12 Continuity and Change

What was new about Fascism was the 'totalitarian' state, and the single party with a mass membership and organisations connecting the people to the State. This was Fascism's 'new order', but it never really came into being, and the Fascist regime is probably best understood as a kind of compromise, a living together or power-sharing arrangement between this Fascist 'new order' and the country's established institutions, which co-operated in and survived Fascism's coming to power. Mussolini expected that with the passing of the generations, the organisations of the 'totalitarian' state, through its control of young people, for instance, would eat away at the hold of institutions like the Catholic Church. He thought that successful wars would strengthen Fascism's standing in Italy and so allow him to speed up the process of reducing the power of bodies to which many Italians still felt attached. In conversations with his Foreign Minister and son-in-law, Galeazzo Ciano, in the late 1930s, Mussolini looked forward to a settling of accounts with the Church and the monarchy once the anticipated war was won.

The Post-war Anti-Fascist Republic

But the war was lost, of course, and Fascism's military defeat, the foreign occupation of Italy and the part played in the liberation of the country by the anti-Fascist Resistance movement between 1943 and 1945, seemed to mark the final defeat of Fascism and make possible a clean break with the Fascist period. In a real sense, this actually happened. The political system changed from a Fascist dictatorship to a democratic parliamentary republic, formally brought into being with the 1948 constitution. More than that, as political parties re-formed during and after the war, the basis of co-operation and unity between them for the country's post-war reconstruction was anti-Fascism. The constitution banned and made illegal the reorganisation of a Fascist party, and the Socialist, Communist and Catholic Christian Democratic parties worked together in coalition governments between 1945 and 1947. The Italian Communist party, which became one of the largest in Western Europe, consistently gaining between a quarter and a third of the popular vote, built its post-war political strategy around anti-Fascism. It did not seek to carry out a Bolshevik-like revolution, but decided to build on the 1943-5 experience when it had fought alongside other groups in the political and military Resistance against the Fascists of the Salò republic and their German allies, and work with the democratic parties to install and defend a progressive, reforming republican and parliamentary system of government.

The Communist party was, in effect, permanently excluded from government in 1947, with the onset of the Cold War in Europe, and thereafter coalition governments were dominated by the Christian Democrats. Even though anti-Communism became the cement of the Italian coalition governments which were formed in the late 1940s and 1950s especially, the Cold War climate did not provide the opportunity for a Fascist revival. The Christian Democratic party was conservative and anti-communist, but was still committed to the parliamentary republic, and the dominant party's stance left little room for the neo-Fascist party which had been formed in 1946, the Italian Social Movement or MSI. In 1960, a right-wing Christian Democrat-led government won a vote of confidence in parliament with the support of the MSI deputies, but fell shortly after in the wake of popular and political outrage at what had happened, a confirmation that the anti-Fascist political agreement still existed.

The rebuilding of domestic politics on an anti-Fascist foundation was matched by changes to Italy's external relations. Nationalism and imperialism were no longer the inspiration for a foreign policy of greatness and expansion. Under its post-war democratic governments, Italy stopped even pretending to be an aspiring great power and found a place in international (NATO) and European (EEC) networks dominated by others.

Neo-Fascism

The MSI was the most evident sign that Fascism still lived on in some form, though many observers thought that its relatively low key electoral performance (2 per cent of the national vote in the 1948 elections, rising to 9 per cent in the 1972 elections), indicated that Fascism was a spent force. The MSI took its name and inspiration from the so-called Italian Social Republic, the Fascist puppet government of German-occupied northern and central Italy in 1943-5, but was never prosecuted as a Fascist organisation under the terms of the 1948 constitution. Within the MSI were groups who wanted a more authoritarian system of government and were prepared to use violence to achieve it, as well as groups who wanted to work through the parliamentary system and make the MSI a respectable conservative party. The anti-system neo-Fascists had a hand in the so-called 'strategy of tension' in the 1970s when, in response to student and worker protest and unrest in the late 1960s, acts of terrorism aimed to make the country unstable and support the case for the introduction of 'strong' government to put an end to the instability. By the 1980s, however, the MSI was positioning itself as a conservative constitutional party, and with the collapse of Communism in Eastern Europe, the end of the Cold War, and the break up of the Christian Democratic party, it actually became a party of government again in the early 1990s. Renamed the National Alliance, and claiming that it was 'post-Fascist', the party won 13 per cent of the vote and 100 seats in the 1994 elections, and joined the short-lived government led by the Rupert Murdoch-like figure, Silvio Berlusconi, the head of a vast media business empire and owner of the Milan soccer club. Mussolini's granddaughter, Alessandra, was elected to parliament for the National Alliance in 1994, nearly 50 years after her grandfather had last held some form of power.

The Hidden Fascist Legacy

The neo-Fascist groups involved in the terroristic acts of the 1970s had some support and connections among the State's civilian and military officials, especially senior men in the country's secret police and armed forces intelligence services. Some have seen this kind of complicity of some state officials in subversive activity as a sign of Fascism's hidden legacy to the post-war parliamentary republic. This was a reactionary and authoritarian 'culture' persisting among senior civil servants, judges, and armed forces officers whose careers and those of their immediate predecessors had developed during the Fascist period and in the service of the Fascist state. It is difficult to measure the extent of such a set of attitudes among Italy's public employees. But it might show a basic continuity in the running of the State's bureaucracy from liberal Italy, through the Fascist period and into the democratic republic. The Fascist regime only got so far in 'Fascistising' the personnel and methods of the civil service it inherited from Giolitti and, to a large extent, the State apparatus operated as it had done before, an indication of that cohabitation between the Fascist 'new order' and members of the country's existing establishment characterising much of the Fascist period. While there was in 1945-6 every intention to get rid of state officials compromised by their service of the Fascist state, such a large scale purge never happened. This was partly because so many civil servants had joined the Fascist party as a matter of course, making it too difficult to determine the quality of their involvement with the Fascist regime, and partly because after war and occupation the government needed an experienced state administration to help the country through post-war reconstruction. So the post-war democratic governments of Italy continued to be serviced by a state machine which had done its duty by the preceding Fascist regime.

Institutional Continuity

This issue of a continuity in institutions can be taken further. The monarchy was the one big institutional victim of the change from Fascism to democracy and paid for its co-existence with Fascism in the special referendum of 1946, when Italians voted narrowly to abolish the monarchy. But other institutions survived unreformed and prospered after 1945. Judges continued to apply the codes of civil and criminal law which had been drawn up by the Fascist government in the early 1930s, and proposals for revising them were finally made only in the 1960s. The 1948 constitution did not commit itself one way or another on the kind of economic system Italy should have after the war,

82

and certainly the idea of wholesale nationalisation and state control looked too much like the Fascist state's attempted regulation of the economy. The flow of American money to pay for Italian post-war economic reconstruction and Italy's place in the Western bloc during the Cold War division of Europe, ensured that it would be a capitalist economy. But the constitution's non-committal stance meant that the mixed part privately-run and part publicly-run economy carried on, and that included the state-owned or state-controlled economic agencies and enterprises of the Fascist period, such as IRI.

The single most important national institution to make the transition from Fascism to democracy intact was the Catholic Church. The Pope thought that the Concordat of 1929 both protected and advanced the position of the Church in Italian society and within the Fascist state, where it operated as a semi-independent body and enjoyed legal rights, over marriage for instance, which would probably never have been normally granted in negotiations with a democratic parliamentary government. The expectation was that the Concordat would be abolished after the final defeat of Fascism. But far from being ended, the Concordat, which gave the Catholic Church a privileged status in Italian life, was included in the 1948 constitution. The left-wing parties and, above all, the Communist party, felt that to abolish the Concordat was to risk a dangerous conflict between Church and State, and would undermine the unity of anti-Fascist forces, including the Catholics, which had been behind the Resistance and now was the basis of the new republic. Basically, the communists backed the keeping of the Concordat in order to ensure that Catholics and the Christian Democrat party would back democracy. The Catholic Church, because it was the sole non-Fascist body allowed to operate in the 1930s, had become by the fall of Fascism the only nationwide institution capable of replacing the mass organisations of the Fascist party. Most of the leaders of the post-war Christian Democratic party and of the networks of Catholic bodies which supported the political dominance of that party after 1948, had been educated in Catholic colleges and universities and were members and leaders of Catholic Action during the 1930s and early 1940s. The Concordat had allowed the Church to fence off a generation of Catholics from whose ranks came the political class of post-war Italy, and so in a very concrete way, it was one of Fascism's most significant handovers to the Italian post-war republic. The Catholic Church's hold over many aspects of Italian life was eroding from the 1960s, as religious practice declined and society's values became more secular, in other words, less affected by religion and by what the Church said and believed, a consequence of the so-called 'economic miracle' of the late 1950s and 1960s when tens of thousands of Italians migrated from rural areas to work in the expanding towns and industries of northern Italy. No Concordat, whether made in a Fascist or a democratic context, could protect the Church from the secularisation of society in a country which was fast becoming a modern industrial nation.

Glossary

Azione Cattolica Italiana

The network of Catholic organisations initially created in the late nineteenth century to defend the interests of the Catholic Church and religion in the new state of Italy, and later in Fascist Italy.

Alleanza Nazionale

The name adopted by the present-day neo-Fascist party in Italy.

Autarchy

The policy which aimed to achieve Italy's economic self-sufficiency, formally adopted as a goal by the Fascist regime in the mid-1930s.

Axis, Rome-Berlin

The phrase first used by Mussolini in 1936 to describe the co-operative relationship between Fascist Italy and Nazi Germany.

Biennio rosso

The term, meaning 'Red Two Years', which contemporaries used to describe the apparently revolutionary social and economic popular agitation of 1919-20.

Democrazia Christiana

The name of the dominant post-1945 political party in Italy, the Christian Democratic party, and of the Catholic political ideas which lay behind it and its predecessor, the Popular party of 1919-26.

Duce

The term which means 'leader', coming from the Latin word *dux*, and which was applied to Mussolini as the head of Fascism and of the Italian people, and used to build up the cult of the 'totalitarian' leader from the mid-1920s.

84

Fasci di combattimento	Literally 'combat' or 'fighting groups', the name given to the local units of organisation of the Fascist movement from 1919; the word fascio was used in Italian politics before Fascism, mainly on the left, and conveyed the sense of a looser association than a political party.
Istituto di Ricostruzione Industriale	The public body set up in 1933 by the government to rescue banks and industries hit by the Depression, through which the State came to control large sectors of Italian industry.
Movimento Sociale Italiana	The neo-Fascist party founded in 1946 by a group of ex-Fascists involved in the Salò Republic.
Partito Comunista Italiana	The Italian Communist party, founded in 1921.
Partito Nazionale Fascista	The National Fascist party, formed in 1921 and dissolved in 1943.
Partito Popolare Italiano	The Italian Popular party, the democratic Catholic party formed in 1919 and dissolved in 1926.
Partito Socialista Italiano	The Italian Socialist party, founded in 1892.
Risorgimento	The term for the nineteenth century Italian national political and cultural revival which culminated in the unification of the country by 1870.
Trasformismo	The term used to describe the practice of 'transforming' political opponents into supporters, of bringing former opponents into the orbit of government.

Further Reading

1. General Textbooks Covering the Whole Period

C. Seton-Watson *Italy from Liberalism to Fascism, 1870-1925* (London: Methuen, 1967) is long in the tooth, but still a good old-fashioned political narrative. M. Clark's excellent *Modern Italy, 1871-1982* (London: Longman, 1984) covers both 'high' and 'low' politics and is good on economic, social and cultural developments, too.

2. The Fascist Period

After a long gap following E.R. Tannenbaum's *Fascism in Italy. Society and Culture, 1922-43* (London: Allen Lane, 1973) and A. Lyttelton's *The Seizure of Power. Fascism In Italy, 1919-29* (London: Weidenfeld and Nicolson, 1973), a minor explosion of recent English language general books on Italian Fascism, including D. Thompson *State Control in Fascist Italy: Culture and Conformity, 1925-43* (Manchester: Manchester University Press, 1991), P. Morgan *Italian Fascism, 1919-1945* (Basingstoke: Macmillan, 1995), and J. Whittam *Fascist Italy* (Manchester: Manchester University Press, 1995). The best short treatments are M. Blinkhorn *Mussolini and Fascist Italy* (London: Methuen, 1984), and the really compressed comparative look at Italian Fascism and German Nazism by A. De Grand, *Fascist Italy and Nazi Germany: the Fascist 'Style' of Rule* (London: Routledge, 1995).

D. Mack-Smith's *Mussolini* (London: Weidenfeld and Nicolson, 1981) is the English language biography of the Fascist dictator, very different from the De Felice treatment. The De Felice controversy can be picked up in R.J.B Bosworth's two historiographical books, *Explaining Auschwitz and Hiroshima. History Writing and the Second World War* (London: Routledge, 1990) and *The Italian Dictatorship. Problems and Perspectives in the Interpretation of Mussolini and Fascism* (London: Arnold, 1998), as well as in the uncritical article by M. Ledeen, 'Renzo de Felice and the Controversy over Italian Fascism', *Journal of Contemporary History* 11 1976, and in the rather more critical ones by B.W. Painter, 'Renzo De Felice and the Historiography of Italian Fascism', *American Historical Review* 95 1990, and M. Knox, 'The Fascist Regime, its Foreign Policy and its Wars: an Anti-Anti-Fascist Orthodoxy?' *Contemporary European History* 4 1995.

Index

Primary references are in **bold** type

Other titles in the acclaimed Sempringham Studies series
with their skilful blend of analysis and clear narrative

Germany 1916-1941 by E.J. Feuchtwanger
140 pp. 5 maps. 15 tables. 10 illustrations. £5.99

Russia 1917-1941 by Martin McCauley
122 pp. 4 maps. 8 tables. 11 illustrations. £5.99

Britain 1916-1940 by Andrew Thorpe
108 pp. 3 maps. 14 tables. 13 illustrations. £5.99

Eastern Europe 1918-1953 by Paul Lewis
140 pp. 5 maps. 7 tables. Illustrations. £5.99

ALSO PUBLISHED BY SEMPRINGHAM

The Good History Students' Handbook
Edited by Gilbert Pleuger
178 pp. 15 tables and illustrations. £5.99

Essays on German History 1862-1939
76 pp. 12 illustrations and maps. £5.99

Landmark essays, by eminent authors, chart the development of Germany
from Bismarck to the rise of Hitler and the outbreak of war in 1939.

Undergraduate History Study - The Guide to Success
This guide which includes sections on undergraduate History study skills
and the theory of History has been widely praised.
92 pp. 20 illustrative figures. £5.99

Sempringham Books are available from bookshops or (postage free) direct from the publisher.

Schools and colleges are offered 10 per cent discount
on orders of 10 or more of the same title
when ordered direct from the publisher

Sempringham Books PO Box 248, Bedford MK40 2SP Tel 01234 267856